# 'I want you to get up out of your seat'

## THELMA SANGSTER

KINGSWAY PUBLICATIONS

EASTBOURNE

ISBN 0 86065 285 8

*Cover photo: Russ Busby, Billy Graham Evangelistic Association*

Printed in Great Britain for
KINGSWAY PUBLICATIONS LTD
Lottbridge Drove, Eastbourne, E. Sussex BN23 6NT by
Richard Clay (The Chaucer Press) Ltd, Bungay, Suffolk.
Typeset by Nuprint Services Ltd, Harpenden, Herts.

# Contents

# *Foreword*

When Billy Graham issues his famous invitation to 'get up out of your seat' miracles take place. Let's be clear—Billy doesn't work those miracles. God does! At the heart of all that Christians believe is a conviction that God has the power to change people's lives.

I've read and heard many testimonies to conversion in my life and so often they take the form of a 'wicked' past leading up to conversion and a happy-ever-after conclusion. What marks this book out for me is that Thelma Sangster goes the other way about. We see here the stories *since* those conversion moments, and this is far more important. For one thing it shows that becoming a Christian isn't a ticket to what the world would think was 'happy ever after'. It is an entry into what St Paul called both a race to be run and a fight to be fought. The point is that in this case it's the *right* race and the *right* fight! Most people, I believe, are running and fighting in the wrong directions—that's the sadness of it all.

But this book does something else important. It shows that it is not 'statistical units of humanity' who get up out of their seats at Billy Graham meetings—it is *lives*. When Billy addresses the 'inquirers' who have come forward to stand in front of the platform he is looking down on hundreds of untold stories. We live in the centre of relationships and we enter into new ones all the time. That means every person changes the world a little bit.

This book brings out how responding to Billy's famous invitation has changed the world, and one would have to be a very distorted person not to admit that the world has been changed for the better.

To me this is the greatest value of Billy Graham, or for that matter any evangelist, whether he or she speak to thousands or ones-and-twos. They change the world for the better. Their ministry is used by God to release people with new life and caring purposes into the twisted and tragic fabric of sinful human society.

Mankind has many problems and some need more working out than can come from the necessarily simple statements of an evangelist. Nevertheless at the heart of all our problems is an inner wrong direction and a rebellion against the loving and just purposes of our Creator. We all need forgiveness and a new life drawing on the resources of the Holy Spirit. This book shows how some people have entered into this experience.

I hope this book will do more than tell the stories of other people. I hope it will change for the better the as-yet-untold stories of many of its readers!

GAVIN REID
*National Director,*
*Mission England*

'We have never seen a moment like this before. It is God's moment—not an end but a beginning' (Billy Graham).*

# 1

## Decision Man

Billy Graham came to London in 1954 as a relatively unknown American evangelist. By the time he finished his twelve-week crusade at Harringay he was an international figure abroad and a household word here in Britain. In those bleak post-war years we had never before seen his like.

His success was not merely the result of a publicity campaign aimed at London's masses, the choice of a huge secular auditorium for the meetings, the combination of talents around him, the willingness of evangelicals to be involved—these factors simply created the opportunities. It was the farm boy from Charlotte, North Carolina, who seized the hour and maximized it, with a fervency and zeal reminiscent of Moody or Spurgeon. A positive catalyst for change, he played the role of God's ambassador to powerful figures (the Prime Minister, Sir Winston Churchill, met him, and was secretly very impressed;[1] the Archbishop of Canterbury, the Lord Mayor of London, and Members of Parliament appeared on the platform at

*Wembley, May 1954.

the final meeting). He was God's agent to vast numbers of ordinary people (the total round figure for attendance topped 2 million).[2] He captured the imagination of a generation indifferent to the church and introduced many people to the reality of God.

What Billy Graham said on his platform was not new—though it was to many in his audience. He restated in simple, dramatic and authoritative terms the biblical concept of a God of utmost holiness. Here was an uncompromising God, bigger than any model in the current liberal 'demythologizing' mode, who offered forgiveness and life to mankind in the death and resurrection of Jesus Christ, asked for commitment and obedience, and promised assurance and peace through the Holy Spirit and the working of the word. Billy resisted the temptation to philosophize about religion, or try to impress people, and his burning evangelical conviction challenged the prejudices of entrenched theological positions.

Billy used for background a vast cosmic canvas of events, a worrying world rather more detached from his hearers' perceptions than is today's global village. The Bikini atoll hydrogen bomb test had just occurred, unleashing new powers of destruction. Billy spoke to New Elizabethans still battle-weary from the past, fearful of the communist menace in the present and uncertain about a future with the Bomb. He told them what was wrong—man himself was out of control. He told them what they needed to fill the void left by the pursuit of material solutions. 'The Bible says...'—it was the answer to every problem, however 'simplistic' it might seem.

He used his considerable natural powers to dramatize the message. Even with the lapse of thirty years those present can recall the 'film star' impact of the tall athletic figure, the blond good looks, but mainly the voice, falling, rising, climbing to its objective. It was the cry of the prophet, urging the people to repent, the instrument of the surgeon, probing the conscience; it called to old and young, with the fire and energy of a man in the prime of life, to come and make peace with God. There was no hysteria, but there was a compulsion present. As Eric Delve, who heard and is now himself an evangelist, says: 'The message was in the voice. The voice *was* the message. Here you had a man called to call. He was God's great reaper where others had sowed.'

The Bishop of London, Dr Wand, sat on the platform at one crusade meeting. Next day someone asked his opinion. He replied, 'I could have preached a better sermon—but no one would have come forward when I had finished!'[3]

The press, which had whipped up an anti-Billy campaign even before he landed, decided in the end that here was a phenomenon that could not be dismissed as American razzmatazz or 'mass hypnotism', and ultimately the publicity did him more good than harm.

'I never knew simplicity could cudgel us sinners so damned hard,' wrote Cassandra of the *Daily Mirror*, after a famous interview with Billy in the pub 'The Baptist's Head'.

The procedures for follow-up of inquirers involved counsellor training and the co-operating churches were asked to send suitable people. An advertisement explained what was happening to the Christian public at large: 'Billy Graham always insists on the wholehearted support of the churches, and he gets it because his follow-up organization is as comprehensive as it is efficient.'[4]

The inquirers were to be put in touch with a church of their own choice, or else be designated to one by a committee representing all denominations. The Billy Graham organization thus made it clear that the nurturing of the converts was the job of the churches. But the churches were largely unprepared for such an influx of converts. The 38,000 responses from the Harringay crusade surprised even the Billy Graham team, and a blizzard of inquirers' cards clogged the referral system.[5] Other problems arose. In an effort not to over-influence church preferences, and to respect geographical, particularly Anglican parish boundaries, some live 'chicks' were put under dead 'hens'. Numbers of inquirers who had not found their way to live church fellowships and still had unanswered problems started writing in to a follow-up department that could not expand sufficiently to cope.

Arthur Coe was to become general secretary of Contact for Christ Service, a nationwide counsellor and follow-up ministry, as a direct result of the influence of his initiation into counselling at Harringay. He has said: 'Where there is thorough follow-up of the individual into small fellowship groups, then there is success. Where this is neglected then many become casualties of the enemy. In the parable of the sower it was the birds of the air who took away the seed.'

Without diminishing what was achieved, it must be assumed that, in a situation that was totally new to the churches and on such a scale, many inquirers must have slipped through butter-fingers. Some, as seen in this book, found other 'catchers'. Where a real work of grace was done, people were not left high and dry. However, lessons were learned for future crusades—and Mission England strategy is the result. Instead of a crusade which starts in the centre and works out to the churches in by-products and spin-offs, Mission England starts in the churches, and over a three year period is encouraging them, by means of a training programme, to do their own evangelism, using the crusade as a stimulus. The crusade is being held in five regions of England, with a short campaign by Billy himself as a central feature. 25–30% of the churches in Britain are involved.

One of the most heartening features of the Harringay crusade, however, was the impact it had on clergy and ministers, 80% of whom co-operated with the Greater London crusade. One ex-missionary in charge of a neighbouring cause was so impressed by the change in his young people that he went to Harringay to see for himself. Within a few days he remarked, 'I have put away my books, so that I may study and preach the Bible!'[6]

Besides Harringay—which included a huge rally in Hyde Park attended by 45,000 people on Good Friday—there were hastily convened relay services through post office landlines, to a nationwide audience of listeners in theatres, concert halls, auditoriums and churches, an approach that was to be widely used in later crusades. There were meetings with major groups of people and every Sunday was filled. On April 25th Billy paid a visit to Cambridge and preached in the packed university church, Great St Mary's, with the service relayed to two neighbouring churches. Among those who responded were two young history students, who now play a key role in the Birmingham Bible Institute—its chaplain, Bob Dunnett, and his wife Diana.

Bob has commented, 'For Diana it was the culmination of several years of great conviction, for me, of just a few months. For both of us it was deep, making an immediate change in our life and standards and giving full assurance of having met God. Within two years an unmistakable call had come to the ministry. I was in training at Oak Hill Theological College and Diana was at Mount Hermon Bible College.'

The grand climax came on May 22nd when Billy spoke before 67,000 people in White City Stadium, with an overflow in nearby Queen's Park Rangers football ground, and before a massive crowd of 120,000 in Wembley

Stadium, when 2,000 people responded.

Had London, Britain even, turned to God? The glorious hope receded. But nothing could ever be exactly as it was before. God was now on the agenda for open discussion, and Christians had found their tongues. Churches had been awakened, and were experiencing what it was to work together in evangelism. The converts themselves began to move into avenues of service and the theological and Bible training colleges were to feel the impact. Bob Dunnett feels, 'The 1954 Crusade produced a new generation of Christians. I have met Billy's converts everywhere. A great many went into full-time service. The work that was done at Harringay was a deep work. In the parable of the sower the Lord puts the emphasis on the soil.'

Billy came next to the Kelvin Hall, Glasgow, Scotland, in 1955, where the crusade was part of the ongoing 'Tell Scotland' movement. Congregations were dwindling and in many pulpits the liberal voice had undermined biblical authority. Could the Harringay experience be repeated in Scotland? They hardly dared to think so. In fact, it was *bettered* statistically. 'Scotland had rediscovered that religion was "the most important and exciting thing in the world—more exciting and more vital than a Cup final",' reported *The Christian* at the close.[7]

Two and a half million attended and more responded (52,000 people) in six weeks than had the previous year in twelve weeks. The relays to forty towns in Easter week made it an All-Scotland crusade, and in the last two weeks 1,560 separate relays went to towns in the rest of the country.

There was a final week at Wembley Stadium in May. It rained hard for all but two nights out of seven but half a million people came and around 3,000 inquirers each night found their way across the turf. On the night that

Helen Macintosh found what she was seeking—then just a face in a rain-soaked crowd—the Duchess of Kent was in the Royal Box accompanied by her sister, Princess Olga. Billy had already met the Queen Mother and Princess Margaret, and was to preach before the Queen at Windsor. Royalty recognized the importance of what was happening, even if many church leaders at this stage ignored it.

Dr C. T. Cook wrote in *The Christian* on Friday, May 27th, that the 'signs following' the crusades of the two years included increased attendances at churches and more conversions from the ministers' preaching: 'Ministers and members... have seen God at work in response to prayer and faith on a scale they hardly thought possible in these days. They are experiencing a breath of revival.'

One such minister, the Rev. G. Maurice Marks, was then in charge of a Congregational church in Barrhead, a small industrial community on the outskirts of Glasgow. Three years later, he had moved out to a church in Kingston, Jamaica, where he became chairman of a committee preparing for Billy Graham's visit to that island. There he told what had happened at Barrhead as a result of the All-Scotland crusade. Over 100 people in his church had committed themselves to Christ, some at the crusade, others who were not able to attend the meetings had done so in his vestry or the manse, but mostly it happened *after* the crusade was over:

'One Sunday morning, I remember, I was led to do something I had never done before; something that just wasn't done in our churches in Scotland. At the close of the sermon I invited those who wished to commit themselves to Christ to leave their seats and come forward to the Communion table. Fifty-two people of all ages from 15 to 60 responded to the appeal. Others followed their example as the weeks went by...the Holy Spirit did the work very thoroughly. You would have to be a Scot to realize how much it cost them to make that public confession.'[8]

In 1961 Main Road Stadium, Manchester, was the scene of the three-week crusade. There were 2,000 relays. Half a million people attended the Manchester crusade and 40% of the almost 18,000 inquirers were aged between 15 and 18.

Billy came twice more to Britain on the evangelism trail—to Earls Court in 1966 and 1967. It was the age of the Beatles and the Stones, symptomatic of the anarchism and rebellion of the young against authority and history. The message from the platform was undiluted by trendiness. It met a deep hunger. It was timeless. The proportion of those who responded with no church background was higher than at Harringay. Cliff Richard appeared on the Earls Court platform in 1966 to testify to his faith. It was the television era and one month's crusade in 1966 with televised relays in ten centres produced a million attendances and 45,000 inquirers. Nine days in the following year, with televised relays in twenty-five regional centres turning it into an All-Britain crusade, drew another million and produced more than 34,000 inquiries. The relays did have their hazards. In *The Times* it was mentioned that the 1966 audiences watching their 30-foot high screens saw a 2-foot fly on Billy's collar at one point.

One paper unable to deny the scale of the drama being played out in the crusade swung a punch: 'The chief danger from Billy Graham's crusaders is that they might succeed in putting people off organized religion even more than they are already.'[9]

There was little fear of that happening. John Pollock[10] records that in 1966, 'Scores of counsellors were fruit of '54 and '55 and one evening thirty-one young ministers, all crusade converts, sat together while a spokesman gave their testimony.'

The Bishop of Norwich, the Right Reverend Maurice Wood, principal of Oak Hill Theological College from 1961–71, said in 1983: 'I would say that during the ten years I was principal I never had less than 10% of the Church of England ordinands who had not been converted through Billy Graham's ministry.... During the Earls Court crusade we made contact with the theological colleges and the missionary colleges, and one night we had seventy young men and women in a block, witnessing to the fact that their commitment to Christ had led on to training for whole time service to Christ's church at home and abroad.'

In the years since Billy started campaigning, calls have come to him from all over the world—he has held meetings in Europe, India, the Caribbean, Australasia, Africa, the Middle East, South America, Canada, Central America, Japan, Korea, the Far East, and behind the Iron Curtain in Hungary, Poland, Russia and Czechoslovakia. His stature has grown with the years. He has addressed 92 million people and his team has recorded almost 2 million inquirers. Many more went unrecorded.

The figures sound impressive, but how many of these inquirers stayed the course? By no means all would have totally understood the message, would have found the right churches to get further help, or have kept the flame alive. Yet surveys done after the early crusades showed a surprisingly large number soldiering on, and ten years after Harringay, limited advertising in the Christian press produced 600 replies. The files of the Billy Graham Evangelistic Association in Minneapolis tell a continuing story and *Decision* magazine publishes a constant stream of testimonies, mostly from the USA. Five years after a crusade, it has been said, the inquirers are still finding their way to the churches. The Holy Spirit is able to finish what has been begun.

That the crusades in Britain transformed the evangelical cause, giving it new power and confidence cannot be doubted. Canon Harry Sutton, former general secretary of the South American Missionary Society, now Canon Missioner of the Society, who, in the last two or three years visited twenty-three different countries, says: 'Wherever I have travelled around the world, I have been intrigued to discover men and women serving Christ and the Church as a result of first coming to know the Saviour at a Billy Graham crusade.

'God has undoubtedly used Billy Graham, not only in the conversion of men and women who have served their own generation locally, but also to the uttermost parts of the earth in the most difficult and needy corners of the vineyard.'

But it is also true that membership of the major Protestant churches has declined by as much as 43% since Harringay.[11] About one thousand churches closed in the 1970s and the ministry was reduced by 2,500. The crusades could not permanently arrest this decay, which was governed by many outside factors. Yet one important long-term effect of the earlier crusades was to put people into positions of Christian service where they could enable the church to cope with the situation of decline and promote an upturn. Some of these people's stories are included in this book. The National Director of Mission England, Gavin Reid, comments: 'Any undeniable overall decline has to be balanced against a considerable number of church attenders who owe their conversion to Billy Graham's ministry.'

The testimonies in the chapters that follow demonstrate lucidly the reality of that key statement on Crusade banners: 'Jesus says I am the Way, the Truth and the Life'

(Jn 14:6). These were young people, none over the age of 30, and mainly under 20. With their choices still before them they stood, unknown faces in a crowd at the foot of a platform, but representing the church's future. What would they become?

They all needed and wanted in varying degrees an ultimate reality, the truth about themselves and their destiny. They found truth, life and purpose in Jesus. From the hub that was Harringay, Kelvin Hall, Wembley, Manchester or Earls Court their paths radiated out in service, touching and changing many other lives *en route*.

Through careers, marriages, successes and failures, illness, accidents and death, these lives show the existence of a divinely creative large-scale plan, which works through belief and commitment to bring order out of seeming chaos, and rest to the questioning human heart. Their disappointments have proved to be 'his appointments', their fulfilments were not for themselves alone—they have also built up the church, in its many manifestations, and brought health to the wider society. In their variety they speak to us of the many-sided nature of God who makes us in his image. They were saved to serve and are thus symbolic of all that is best about Billy's mission. They teach us what God can do with anyone who will give him room to work.

These stories also teach something about 'the church' that we are inclined to forget—that it is one body. To bring these lives to himself and help them grow God has used different parts of the network of interlocking systems that we call 'The Church'. Sometimes, sadly, they have been hindered by a 'small corner' mentality which puts doctrine before love. If we were not so determined to work in dislocation, think what power the body would have to bring a new generation to the birth.

These stories also give primary insights into the evolutionary changes in society generally over the past three decades. They are about people of a time and place and social attitude. Some have their own tribal languages and customs—and for observing tribes, London or the North-East can be as good vantage points as the Amazon jungle. The message which Billy Graham preaches crosses the barriers and borders, and cracks open human indifference.

Billy Graham has never been short of critics. His attitude to the communist world,[12] to ecumenicism,[13] his 'fascination with politics',[14] the tactics of mass evangelism—which includes literature, radio and film ministries—and his 'superstar' status have all fuelled the fires of criticism. A man who has preached to more people than any other evangelist alive or dead and on a world-wide scale offers a huge target to all-comers. His best defence is that lives have been salvaged and new works brought to birth. That the word Billy proclaims has not lost its power over the years can be judged by the fact that when he came to Blackpool in 1982 for two nights, 1,000 people responded to the invitation.

Mission England brings him once more—possibly for the last time—in a major crusade. This time imaginative training measures will do what is humanly possible to conserve the fruits. When the big event passes, the aim is that the strengthened local church will bring up the new converts, in turn to be rejuvenated by them—a new church for a new age.

Gavin Reid has said: 'There is a place for the big and dramatic event. Why else did Jesus ride publicly and triumphantly into Jerusalem? He knew that in the big dimensions of his time the people had to face the challenge of turning to him or rejecting him.'[15]

Writing this book has brought back a buried memory. As a young and hard-pressed missionary editor of an outreach magazine, *Caribbean Challenge*, I interviewed

Billy Graham on a Jamaican hotel verandah, before his Latin American tour in 1962. I was desperately in need of a story, rather in awe of him. He, without in the least conveying that I was interrupting precious time for quiet, granted me the interview, and told how he and Harold Wildish, the leading Brethren evangelist and teacher, had distributed copies of *Caribbean Challenge* to jet-setting patrons of that hotel. We were sharers, he implied, in a common task. I went away, reinforced to fight another day. Thanks, Billy.

Thanks also to many unnamed people who made a contribution to this book. A particular thank you to the subjects themselves, who patiently and honestly answered so many probing questions; especially Eric Delve, who generously gave time during the Mission to London; to Maurice Rowlandson, director of the Billy Graham Evangelistic Association and staff for supplying data; the Reverend Canon Tom Livermore for helpful background information; Arthur Coe of Contact for Christ for suggestions; Reverend Rob Marshall and Peter Collins for research; Mrs Rosemary Armer and Mrs Angela Marshall for typing help; my husband Derek for constructive criticism, and daughters Joanna and Andrea for their support.

## Notes

1. John Pollock, 'Crusades—Twenty Years with Billy Graham' (Billy Graham Evangelistic Association, 1966, 1969), p.141.
2. The majority of the statistics in this chapter are taken from figures issued by the Billy Graham Evangelistic Association, supplemented by other contemporary sources.
3. I am indebted to the Reverend Canon Tom Livermore for these stories.
4. *The Christian*, February 26th 1954. BGEA.
5. Mrs Pauline Young, who handled the cards, says: 'We

worked a twelve-hour day, six days a week. The numbers overwhelmed the organization.'

6.  See note 3.

7.  The Reverend George Young, *The Christian*, May 6th 1955. BGEA.

8.  *Caribbean Challenge*, January 1958 (published by Christian Literature Crusade, Kingston, Jamaica).

9.  *The Inquirer* (Unitarian and Free Christian Weekly), reported in *The Christian*, June 24th 1966.

10.  See note 1.

11.  Tom Houston, writing in *Decision*, March 1983, BGEA.

12.  *Church of England Newspaper*, May 21st 1982.

13.  See, for instance, John Pollock, 'Crusade "66"' (1966), p.83, and 'Graham: A Day in Billy's Life' (1976), p.79 (Hodder & Stoughton).

14.  John Peters, *The Harvester*, September 1983.

15.  *Decision*, April 1983, BGEA.

*'None of us will ever understand all the gospel and all about God. You have to come by faith. Faith means a total commitment to Jesus Christ, and to him alone'* (Billy Graham).

# 2

# *Where God Is, Love Is*

Roy Hicks walked away from Harringay arena on an April night in 1954, feeling that life had suddenly acquired some purpose. He thought over all that had happened since he had slid into a seat to hear the famous evangelist Billy Graham. What he'd said was not entirely new to Roy, but it was the clarity and the certainty of the messenger that had drawn the 14-year-old boy out of his seat to commit himself to Jesus Christ. Now he felt totally care-free, as if walking on air.

Gradually, though, his feelings of elation evaporated. True, he was baptized six months later, but undoubtedly the wonder of it all slowly faded. There were other things on his mind—exams to pass, the world to change through politics, and fun to be had dancing and going to the cinema.

At 19 Roy suddenly woke up to his spiritual poverty. He was attending the Keswick convention in the Lake District. A chat in the counselling tent with Tim Buckley of the London Bible College showed him where he was—a lost sheep, out in the cold, caught in the brambles, at a dead end.

Roy became convinced that he should train for the ministry.

But the London Bible College or Spurgeons? In the end he opted for the former, even though he had a place promised at his denominational college. It was a step of faith, for there was no certainty he would be accepted, or get a grant for the three-year course. On both counts he succeeded, though he suffered other disappointments. He felt instinctively that this was to be the pattern for the future—walking the pathway of faith through a maze of contrary circumstances. He was certainly right on that score.

After graduating from college, Roy took a post at a Christian hotel in Bournemouth. It was some three years later that he received an astonishing telephone call.

The caller was a former guest at the hotel and had the following proposition to make: 'I feel the Lord has told me to buy you a house,' the caller began. 'You can choose within this price range' (he named a figure) 'and live in it rent free for as long as you need to. It can be anywhere you need to be.'

Roy was stunned. Only five minutes before he and his wife, Margaret, were facing life without home or job. They had decided that they could not carry on with their very demanding job in the hotel, as Margaret's health was slowly giving way under the strain. And yet this man, whom they did not know well, had somehow discerned their need. Without a doubt, it was an answer to prayer, but what was the ultimate purpose?

Just three days before they moved into their new home at Wareham in Dorset, they knew the answer: Roy was invited to be part-time pastor at nearby Corfe Mullen Baptist Church. However, it was only two days after Roy had accepted this invitation that he received another from Francis Dixon, the well-known Bible teacher, who asked

Roy to join him at Lansdowne Baptist Church, on a full-time basis. It was an offer Roy would have jumped at, and he was disappointed that it had come too late. Despite this, Roy felt there was a divine purpose in this train of events.

At his induction service the Rev Francis Dixon gave Roy and Margaret a significant verse of Scripture: 'And the hand of the Lord was with them: and a great number believed, and turned unto the Lord' (Acts 11:21, AV). It was a verse that assumed even greater meaning in the weeks and months that followed.

Roy and Margaret were happy at the little church. Its village-sized congregation grew to 150, and people were attracted from far and near. Members of the nearby Post Green Christian community became involved, giving extra vitality to the worship.

It had seemed right to Roy not to ask for a salary; 'I am employed by the Lord, not the church,' he told the deacons. He supplemented his income by teaching religious education at a local secondary school.

Three years went by and then, just as before, without warning, the owner of their house contacted them again, with another proposition:

'I feel this is going to be a year of change for you. Leave the house if you want to, and I will sell it. I'm prepared to buy you another elsewhere on the same terms as before.'

Roy and Margaret looked at one another in surprise. Was God really speaking to them through this man? In just three weeks they knew the answer. A church on the other side of Bournemouth invited Roy to be pastor. The spiritual atmosphere was so arid there that their first reaction was to say no. Two things, however, changed their minds. Roy felt God was drawing his attention to Exodus 33:15: 'If thy presence go not with me carry us not up hence'. The other influence was the remarkably smooth changeover of properties at a time when the property market was lifeless. When they started to look, there was nothing available at the right price or location. Then, for no apparent reason, the name of a former guest at the Christian hotel came to mind. He had arrived one night needing help and friendship, and had ended up moving into the locality. Roy decided to ring him.

'Dreadful cheek, I know, but do you happen to be selling your house?' Roy asked.

'Why, yes. I advertised it last week but I've had no replies.'

In eight years the second church grew from some two dozen to between 200 and 300, and the church premises were practically rebuilt. However, sadly there was a split in the church. Roy tendered his resignation, on the day after Palm Sunday. It promised to be a black Easter.

Roy wondered despondently if his ministry was finished. Then he opened his Bible and the following words stood out: 'Thine ears shall hear a word behind thee, saying, This is the way, walk ye in it, when ye turn to the right hand, and when ye turn to the left' (Is 30:21, AV). A deep peace assured him all was well.

Roy learned that 100 members of his church had also withdrawn, including the secretary, the treasurer, the leader of the women's meeting, the youth leader, and some Sunday school teachers and musicians. They wanted to stay together, with him as their pastor. The situation had all sorts of possibilities for new kinds of ministry but first they needed somewhere to call their own.

Collectively, the new fellowship waited on God for the answer to their problem. Temporary homes were offered by two Anglican parish churches, but the fourth Sunday saw the beginnings of a better answer.

One night, soon after the rift, Roy awoke in the small hours and heard a voice say, quite distinctly:

'Hurn!'

'Hurn?' Roy queried. 'That's only an old airfield. There's nothing there!'

But so strong was the impression that a couple of days later he and others from the newly formed fellowship drove out to Hurn, on the edge of Bournemouth, to look at the airfield. The nearest thing to a village they could find was a post office, a few scattered cottages and the old railway station, now a public house.

Had he imagined the voice in the night? He was sure he hadn't.

They wandered around and, much to their surprise, found a little green-painted wooden chapel hidden in the forest, with a neon sign over the door proclaiming 'God Is Love'. A path cut through the trees to the double door. The little chapel looked forlorn, as if it had come there for a purpose, and then forgotten why.

They walked round it in amazement, and all four were convinced that this was a sign from the Lord. Were they crazy? The building was miles from anywhere, although they noted from the sign outside that it was used for a service on Sunday evenings. They returned home, but they couldn't forget the little chapel. Then Roy realized that he knew the man responsible for the hall—a Christian undertaker.

Two weeks later the group returned to Hurn to look again. Driving home Roy stopped at a phone kiosk to find the undertaker's address. He lived just across the road from the phone box and was, in fact, at home. Roy put his request:

'There are 100 of us needing a place of worship. We saw on the notice board at Hurn that you only have an evening meeting. Is there any possibility of hiring the hall for Sunday mornings?'

The undertaker looked startled. 'Do you know what

I've just done? I've sent in my resignation to all the trustees. My wife and I have been there for thirty years and we just cannot carry on. Only four of us at the most attend, so my wife and I are withdrawing.'

They then learned that the chapel would function for another four weeks and then would be sold—probably for bingo sessions and discos.

The stationmaster at Hurn had built the little hall, they learned, in 1938, when the area was more populated. He held Sunday services in his waiting room at the station until it got too full, when he applied to the landowner for the leasehold to some land. He paid five shillings a year for the lease, and this had never been increased.

The undertaker told Roy and the other fellowship members that if they wished to take over the hall completely his trustees would draw up a new deed and they could appoint trustees of their own.

The group returned to pray over that proposal. When they met a few days later, the Lord seemed to be giving them a clear go-ahead with the words of Micah 7:14: 'Feed thy people with thy rod, the flock of thine heritage, which dwell solitarily in the wood, in the midst of Carmel: let them feed...as in the days of old' (AV).

The little chapel was set in the pine woods, and it was certainly solitary, but they were sure now they should go ahead.

The rent they were charged for the little building—it was only 40 feet by 20 feet—was the original sum mentioned in the deeds: five shillings per annum. And so, within four weeks of leaving their church, the new fellowship set up in the chapel in the woods. Their little refuge, with its neon sign shining out the message 'God Is Love', was nearly full as they met thankfully for that first Sunday service. They gave themselves a name—the Hurn Christian Fellowship.

Almost immediately after this, Roy flew out to Dallas for a Christ for the Nations Seminar. Just as he left, 600 Vietnamese boat people, who had been rescued from the South China Sea by a British ship *Sibonga*, arrived at Sopley camp, 2 miles away from the isolated church. The Fellowship couldn't help but note it—they knew a little about the feeling of being refugees. They wondered if there was some way to help.

Meanwhile, in Dallas, Roy had had a new vision. His ministry until then had been a pastoral one and, some might say, a parochial one. But Christ for the Nations was the place where he became fully aware of the potential of outreach through sponsored churches and individuals all over the world. Roy's eyes opened to the 'harvest fields' outside Britain.

He returned from Dallas in July to receive an exciting message from one of the fellowship who said that she had received a vision in Hurn Fellowship one Sunday morning.

'I saw the church full of Chinese faces,' she told him.

Roy looked hard at her. She was a middle-aged, rather conservative lady who was not given to flights of fancy. It had been a real experience to her.

He remembered it, however, a month later, when he received a call from a Chinese worker connected with Miss Mary Wang and the Chinese Overseas Christian Mission.

The caller said that some of their student workers who could speak both English and Cantonese were at Sopley camp interpreting for the boat people. They were trying to get a Christian service going for the following day but the camp commandant was unable to give them his permission. The little chapel had somehow come to mind.

'Can we bring a few refugees to your morning service?' asked the caller.

'Certainly,' Roy replied, mentally revising his sermon.

'This is wonderful news,' said the voice at the other end of the line. 'There will be about ten, or at the most twenty.'

It was arranged that the Chinese worker, Samuel Cheng, would sit with the Vietnamese in the corner of the church and interpret the service.

By the time Sunday dawned, the Fellowship were wondering what sort of a morning they were going to have. The camp mini-buses rolled up to the door and out poured not ten or twenty, but *one hundred and twenty*, Vietnamese—men, women and children. They flowed in and round the building till the church was filled, then they stood outside, looking through the windows. The order of service went overboard! This one was totally bilingual and punctuated with bursts of laughter and chatter as Samuel Cheng taught the visitors to sing a chorus, featuring the word 'Hallelujah'.

Someone in the congregation had a tape-recorder and captured the precious and historic experience, the dawn of new life for many in the building. The roof threatened to lift off. Those Vietnamese certainly loved to sing. It chased away the blues of camp life.

It was too good for the local press to miss. 'Refugees flood mission hall' ran the headlines.

In the weeks that followed, the staid English at Hurn had to adapt to new ways, and learn to tolerate a noisy crowd. The refugees, upwards of 100 of them on a Sunday morning, jammed in, two or three to a seat, their children round their feet, on the platform, round the walls. It took patience to sit for half an hour while ten-minute messages were translated twice over—into Cantonese and Vietnamese—and to join in the endless singing of simple choruses. But the newcomers added a vital component to the worship—the original congregation could see God was working in human lives before their very eyes. The English heard with delight the first stumbling words of testimony as the refugees began to experience for themselves the wonder of God's love. The little church quickly became known to the boat people as 'The God Is Love Church'. The English fitted in an English-only service in the evening and at other times during the week. As their language improved some of the refugees joined them.

Roy has recalled those early days with the refugees:

'The little wooden chapel set in the trees proved just right for the refugee work. It did not overpower them—it was the type of building they were at home in. It was away from houses, so we could make as much noise as we liked.

'With the refugees we couldn't have solemn services because they were all sad. Anything too solemn would have crushed them. We couldn't teach them complicated hymns, so the singing was all chorus-type. They loved to clap, and the services were bright, mainly gospel, and free. It was thrilling to see them come in, hardly speaking English, loaded with their sorrows and, in a few weeks, see the Holy Spirit at work. Some marvellous testimonies were heard.'

Two weeks after that first Sunday a farmer loaned them a field nearby and they were able to invite the boat people to a big barbecue. It was the start of real friendships between the English and the Vietnamese. From then on the sad, lonely refugees were taken to the hearts of the church family, and given hospitality in their homes.

There was, though, always a sense of urgency about the work with the boat people: they had only three months in which to get people through to an understanding of the gospel and be built up enough to stand on their own feet when they left the camp.

People who visited the huts found themselves crying with the refugees over their terrible problems. Many of them were loaded with very heavy debts. In order to get out of Vietnam they had had to pay gold bars. Some had

borrowed from other refugees and owed thousands of
pounds. Individuals in the church helped some of them to
repay these debts.

As Roy saw it, this was not making 'rice Christians' of
them, but fulfilling the commission he had received in
Dallas, from Isaiah 58—to undo the bands of wickedness,
the heavy burdens, to let the oppressed go free, and break
every yoke. (Often in evangelical circles, Roy feels, the
need for practical love is ignored, when the gospel is
preached. But if love and care are shown the response
comes.)

As the refugees came the church was able to offer—
along with friendship, clothing and hospitality—cassettes
of services, and Bibles. But the expense mounted. As
news spread of what they were doing help arrived from
other quarters. Donations came in and a number of
organizations supported them. Tear Fund gave three
grants over the years; Scripture Gift Mission, the Gideons,
Christ for the Nations and the Bible Society helped with
literature, South East Asia Outreach helped with expenses
and literature; and Chinese Overseas Christian Mission
helped with workers. Three thousand tapes of the church
services were distributed as far afield as Hong Kong,
where a refugee pastor is still using them among refugees.

One young girl of 12 would come and visit the Hicks'
household almost every Sunday. She and her father and
brother had fled from Vietnam, leaving her mother behind.
One day after she had been resettled in Wales she rang
from Christchurch Station:

'I've come to stay with you for a few days,' she said.

When Margaret was putting her to bed that evening she
said, 'Oh, I'm frightened of bed.'

'Why?' asked Margaret.

'Every time I close my eyes I see our next door neighbour at our home in Vietnam,' began the young girl.

Eventually they got the story out of her. One night she had been going to bed when there was a shout from next door. Her father, who was a photographer, was called in, and she went with him. The Vietnamese army had arrived and were torturing the neighbour. Then they shot him. She watched it and her father photographed the scene. From then on, for years in fact, she was unable to sleep, and was terrified of going to bed.

Roy and Margaret prayed that the Lord would heal her memory of these events. She sleeps soundly now. In answer to further prayer her mother was released from Vietnam in July 1983 and is now living with the family in Wales.

Finding their relatives in other countries, or getting them out of Vietnam was and still is the refugees' major anxiety, for the communist government is very loath to let people go. One survivor from the *Sibonga*, Lok Kin Wah —he later took the name Michael Lock—was to marry Julie, a member of the Fellowship who had taught him English. Margaret Hicks traced his three sisters and a boy cousin who had fled separately from Vietnam. Finding them, in Ireland, was a miracle. They arrived at Sopley just in time to attend Michael's wedding. His parents were granted permission to come to England but were turned back from the airport, with no explanation. Michael continued to pray for a miracle, and in May 1983 it happened. His parents, along with another sister, left Vietnam and arrived at Heathrow to make England their new home. In July 1983 they committed their lives to Christ.

The refugees went through Sopley camp in a steady stream for three and a half years. The original idea was that they would be there for three months and then be resettled in other parts of Britain. But the authorities found it harder and harder to get accommodation for their guests. Some were there for eighteen months or two years. The little church touched nearly everybody who passed through the camp, and that meant about 4,000 people. Sadly, some churches in other parts of the country were slower in welcoming the refugees, and consequently some of the boat people found difficulty in standing firm.

In four years 150 people were baptized. It was an act of obedience, which satisfied a deep need in the refugees, who had so little to cling to but God. It was a sign that they were staking their all for Christ, turning from their idols, their gambling habits and their fears.

Some of their prayer requests seemed to demand miracles. One lady stood in the water crying out to God to find her teenage son and daughter and bring them to England. She didn't know whether they were alive or dead. The Fellowship put this need on the prayer list.

Soon after this, the lady left Sopley and went to London. Four months later, Margaret was visiting the camp and knocked on a door. It was opened and there stood the lady, smiling and happy with her two teenage children. They had been intended for another country, but the United Nations organization in charge of allocation had by mistake sent them to England.

On another occasion, Margaret encountered some young men sitting on the grass in the camp and invited them to the services. One was Thi Quoc Hung (renamed Sandy). The young men came to the services, but kept their distance.

One Sunday evening Sandy left Roy and Margaret's house to go to church on the little moped he had bought. At the top of the road he crashed with a car and lay in the road with a dreadful gash on his head.

Roy and Margaret realized that something was wrong as he had not passed them. They turned back and found him lying in the road, groaning. Margaret rushed him to hospital, and it was the care and love he received from the

Christians that convinced him he was part of a family. He committed his life to Christ, and was baptized in 1980. At the baptismal service he told his listeners (by interpretation): 'When we receive the Light of the Lord it is like a mirror—we throw it back to other people. If everybody in all the world could do this and receive the love of the Lord and the love of neighbours, what a wonderful place it would be. We would not have war and cruelty and misery. I would not have to leave my family and wander through the world.'

Sandy set about learning English with such enthusiasm that he became one of the refugees' key interpreters and was responsible for drawing up a very basic Bible course for the Vietnamese.

Sandy had a girlfriend, Nhu, who had gone to America. One day Nhu phoned him from Boston, Massachussetts, where she lived and worked and said she was coming to England. Sandy was both thrilled and troubled. She was not a Christian and therefore he felt he could not marry her.

She came, and soon began to talk about getting married. At the same time she was very opposed to his Christian beliefs. Sandy managed to avoid committing himself to marrying her and when Nhu returned to America he breathed a sigh of relief. However, every Sunday she rang him at Roy's house. Suddenly, some signs of softening appeared in her anti-Christian stance. There was even talk of church. Sandy decided he had better visit her and see what was going on.

Roy and Margaret heard nothing from him at first. Then, two weeks later, the phone rang. It was Sandy with thrilling news. Nhu had been helped to move by one of the Christians from a Boston Baptist church. In conversation he had learned that her boyfriend in England was now a Christian. Without asking her a single question he realized what a predicament Sandy was in. So the Boston church invited her to services and on the day Sandy arrived he found they were all going to a crusade somewhere in Boston. That night Nhu walked forward and gave her life to Christ.

'Wonderful,' said Roy. 'What was the name of the evangelist?'

'Someone called Graham,' came Sandy's reply. He was a little puzzled by the shout of laughter down the phone, until Roy explained that he had just been taken back twenty-nine years. The message hadn't lost its power in the interval.

Two weeks later Roy Hicks arrived in Boston to give Nhu away and to speak for the 'God Is Love Church', Sandy's spiritual home.

For three and a half years hardly a person in the Hurn Fellowship was untouched by the sorrows and joys of the boat people. The family life of Roy and Margaret Hicks and their daughter Deborah was almost totally taken over; and the little fellowship felt bereft when the refugees departed. However, they make forays back to their spiritual base now and again. There are other Vietnamese to be reached throughout Britain, and Roy is developing a travelling ministry with a film of the life of Jesus in Cantonese. Cassettes of the services are in great demand in the Far East.

The Hurn Fellowship get letters practically every day from ex-members of the camp. Some are very involved in serving the Lord and some are sharing Jesus in other parts of the world.

One such letter came from Danh Khoa Duong, a Vietnamese teacher, who had been reunited with his wife and four children in England. He wrote: 'The Lord loves me. He died for me. How great is his love. The most important thing for me now is to be with him eternally. I wasn't alone in my hardships. I came to the Lord in prayer more often and kept my mind on his teachings.'

The feelings of the Hurn Fellowship about the refugees is best summed up by Roy when he says: 'We counted it a joy to serve the Lord in the midst of one of the greatest tragedies in history.'

*'I seemed to hear a voice at my ear saying, "Oh don't go down there. This is not for you—you're Jewish!"'*

# 3

# *The Tug of Love*

Helen Macintosh's story
as told by herself

If I were asked to name the person who has had the greatest influence on my life I would have to say 'Miss Corbett', which is strange, because I only knew her till I was five.

We were a Jewish family living in London. My brother was two years older and my sister six years older than I was. My parents loved me, but did not seem to love each other, and were always bickering and arguing. We children fought too.

Father was an unsuccessful salesman. Mother was a teacher and went out to work, leaving us in Miss Corbett's care. I had a great affection for this lady and she loved me particularly, although she cared for all of us. Her loving disposition stood out in great contrast to all that I saw around me.

Miss Corbett wore old-fashioned black boots—a bit like Mary Poppins. Her hair was scraped back in a bun and she had steel-rimmed glasses, and not a scrap of make-up. She taught us to sing 'All things bright and beautiful', and she must have said something about Jesus because I just knew that he was nice and that he loved little children.

When Miss Corbett left she told my mother she was going to pray for me every day. Years after, my mother showed me letters saying, 'How is Helen? I still pray for her every day.'

At school Jewish children studied only the Old Testament, but I used to hear the others singing their hymns and I knew they were singing about Jesus. I used to think, 'Oh this Jesus—he sounds so nice!'

I asked my mother who Jesus was and she just said, 'It was something political. It's nothing to do with us.' But I couldn't get him out of my mind.

My parents were not Orthodox, but we always kept the Passover. We would sit at a long table with other relatives and Father would say the whole thing in Hebrew, which would make us children giggle...and then we'd be sent out.

We kept the Day of Atonement as well. This is the most solemn day for Jews, when they go to the synagogue and spend twenty-four hours fasting. They are supposed to confess the sins committed through the year and ask God to forgive them. The devout ones beat their breasts. Then they come home in the evening and have a huge meal— and, so it seemed to me, then forget all about it.

I used to insist on fasting, even as a small girl, though children are not obliged to. I wanted to know what things meant—why, for instance, should God care if Jews ate bacon? Maybe the rabbis could have told me, but my parents were too busy with their own problems.

Mum told me Old Testament stories and taught me to say the Shema, which is the prayer every Jew learns to say daily. Jesus would have said it too:

'Hear Oh Israel, the Lord thy God, the Lord is One.'

I said it every night until I was quite grown up. It was

like magic—'If I say this, God will be pleased with me and everything will be all right.'

When I was eleven I won a scholarship to one of the best girls' public schools in England. My mother said to me, 'It's the open door to anything. But if you go there you'll forget about being Jewish and become a Christian, and you won't want to know us.'

It was a very loaded thing to say. I decided I wouldn't go. Instead, I went to Skinner's Company's School for Girls on Stamford Hill, a grammar school which has a very large Jewish population. I was safe there—but I didn't do too well academically. At any rate by 15 I wanted to leave and get a job. Things were difficult at home and I felt I should help.

I got a temporary job in a public library and learned shorthand in the evenings, qualifying in about three months. Then I went into secretarial work.

At the beginning of the war my mother, afraid of bombs, packed us up and moved us to Ruislip. The uprooting upset me because I had just got a boyfriend and was starting to have teenage friends. From then I never had any more Jewish friends. Then I got called up to join the ATS, as a driver.

My brother, rather proud of me, wanted me to have a photograph taken.

The photographer I went to had beautiful portraits in the window of his studio, and had a high reputation. We fell in love.

From then on all I wanted was to get out of the Army and marry Mac. His real name was Dougal, but as he was Scottish he'd been given the usual unoriginal nickname.

I didn't tell my mother at first, because everything about him was wrong, from her point of view. He was twenty years my senior and a divorcee. Worse still, he was a Gentile. It was a bombshell to my parents.

Strangely, Mac was the next person to tell me about Jesus—historical facts, and he would quote things which sounded very wise, adding, 'That's what His Nibs said.'

After we were married I read a book called *The Man Born to Be King*. I was absolutely in tears at the end of it because I knew this man was somebody special, and they'd crucified him. Gentiles brought up with this get inoculated against it, but my reaction was 'How could they do such a thing? He was so beautiful, so noble.' I was very anti-Jewish at that stage.

Our marriage was a difficult one from the start. He had come to it from a bitter divorce. Mac would have preferred us to live together because, he said, marriage spoiled everything. But I insisted on the proper thing. I wanted a son.

Mac's great dream was to have a boat and sail it round the world, not to live in a house. Soon after I met him, he took me with him to buy a sea-going schooner called *Tina*, about 45ft long, with two masts.

When I wanted to have a child he said, 'Well, you know it's going to curtail our freedom. We'll never be able to go away properly.' In the end he came to terms with it—he wanted a son too.

Malcolm's birth, thirteen months after we were married, precipitated a crisis, because we had nowhere to live with our baby except my parents' home. With my parents and my husband hating each other the atmosphere became so unbearable that we had to sell the boat to buy a house. I don't think Mac ever got over that...his whole life's dream sold up to buy a house which he didn't really want.

Mac wanted to have Malcolm baptized, and I was happy for this to be done, though not understanding what it meant. So when he was three weeks old we took him to the local church and he was duly 'done' followed by a party with champagne. What a golden opportunity that vicar missed. No word of explanation—and hungry-hearted me, looking for God.

By the time Malcolm was 2 things had begun to go really wrong with our marriage. It started with the shock of Malcolm's illness at three-and-a-half weeks and his six-week spell in hospital. Then I was ill for about a year with a slipped disc. We had financial problems as well. Mac's business wasn't going as it should because he wasn't very practical about money. I went and got some orders for wedding photographs and I think he resented that I was good at business.

Mac began to go sailing with some new friends on their boat, leaving me at home with Malcolm. I felt neglected, rejected. By the time Malcolm was four I must have been verging on a breakdown. I couldn't cope with the child—he drove me mad. I kept threatening to leave.

I used to send him away to stay with other people now and then to get free of him. When he was naughty I couldn't respond to him with the love and patience he needed, and this made me feel guilty.

I left Mac in 1952. It was a terrible end. I say, 'I left,' but really my husband was pushing me out. He would say, 'Now look, you say you're going. When are you going? You've got to fix a date.' So I left for a job at the Park Lane Hotel. I felt I could cope better on my own than living with the pain of his cold rejection. Mac ran me to the station with my bags.

When I woke up the next morning I thought I'd died and gone to hell. It was August and burning hot in London, without a breath of air. I had left my lovely house and garden in the suburbs and had got this stuffy, dreary little hotel room with taxis honking and belching out petrol fumes all night outside the door.

The job had sounded very high falutin'—secretary to the General Manager—but it consisted only of typing out replies to bookings. I was thoroughly miserable, and cried day and night.

Other jobs followed. I had a terrible time in an Eastbourne hotel. I remember walking along the sea front one February afternoon. The sun was going down over the horizon and blinding me. Suddenly, the thought came: 'I've got to go home. I must go back to my home and child.'

I turned up on the doorstep with my bags. But my husband wouldn't let me stay. I pleaded to be allowed to come back, but he wouldn't have me, not even as a housekeeper.

My heart was broken. I slept on the floor that night, and cried myself to sleep. Then in the morning I crept away, without seeing Malcolm.

I got a job as a secretary in Hammersmith, and I found a room and later a lovely little flat. Unfortunately at this point I met an attractive man and fell in love. He was a bit younger than me, and he didn't want to marry me. It pushed me down even further.

My divorce hearing took place and I lost the custody of Malcolm. He was to be allowed only to come to me on alternate Saturdays—not even to stay the weekend. All this made me feel lower than the dust. I thought, I've ruined my life. Everything's finished!

By this time I had got round to crying to God, night after night, on my knees by my bed. To my mind the only way God could give me back my happiness was to send me another husband so I could have a nice home and be able to see Malcolm more, and provide him with a father figure he could take to. Because this didn't happen and everything went wrong I just felt God was punishing me. I knew I deserved it, but I couldn't take the misery any longer.

I used to lie and look at the gas fire and plan how I was going to end my life. It would be so easy. I would stuff up the doors and turn on the gas. But I always hesitated—arrested by one terrible thought: 'How can I be sure that where I'm going won't be even worse than this?'

In the midst of all this misery, I thought of my mother. Maybe if I put things right with my mother God would stop punishing me. So I rang her up.

She was absolutely marvellous—didn't say anything except, 'Oh, where have you been? I haven't heard from you for such a long time'. (Actually it had been five years!)

She came over to my little flat. She didn't pry. We just chatted. When she had gone I realized that this wasn't the answer. The pain in my heart hadn't eased.

And just then, when I had reached the bottom, Billy Graham came to Harringay. I started seeing posters up everywhere, and read in the papers about people's lives being changed. But I was so wretched I just couldn't believe there was any hope for me. So I didn't go to the crusade.

Life took a turn for the better. I got a good job in Regent Street, and seemed, on the surface, to be doing well. I went to parties, and out drinking and dancing. But underneath I was still desperate.

Then, a year later, I heard that Billy Graham was coming back, to Wembley this time, for a week in May. Ann at my office was also divorced and very unhappy and we agreed to go together. What could we lose?

It was atrocious weather on that Thursday. Ann came in with an excuse. So I was faced with a decision—was I going to hear this madman all on my own on a wet, windy, freezing night? To hear...what? I turned it over in my mind all day long. In the end I went. After all I had tried everything else—why not this?

I stood right up at the back somewhere. I remember the stone steps, the rain blowing in under the roof of the stadium, soaking people. I couldn't see what was going on down there but could hear this choir, and the singing was beautiful. I strained my ears to pick up the words.

Things started to happen down there on the platform. People came on and off. Then someone started speaking, and I supposed it was Billy himself. He was speaking about Pharaoh and the children of Israel—he called him 'Phayroh'.

But I knew all this! I'd heard it since I was knee-high!

Then he began to talk about how Jesus died on the cross and I listened, really arrested. He said, 'There's somebody here tonight carrying a burden of sin and sorrow. It's too heavy for you to bear.' That was me.

He went on, 'Jesus died on the cross for your sins 2,000 years ago and you can leave the burden right here tonight, and go out from this place without it. You can go out with a new life.'

Then he explained that all we had to do was to accept what Christ had already done. It made sense.

I knew I had to make a response of some kind when he said finally, 'It doesn't matter who you are, what you've done, where you are—right up at the back perhaps. If God is calling you, you come. Come to him. Don't let anything keep you from God.'

It was a long, long walk down, and as I went I seemed to hear another voice at my ear saying, 'Oh don't go down there. This is not for you—you're Jewish. You must never have anything to do with Jesus. Though you've committed every sin in the book God will forgive you. But one thing he will never forgive you, and that is for having anything to do with Jesus.'

It was a very persuasive voice, but over it I could hear Billy saying, 'Don't let anything keep you from God'— and I had to go. I knew that what I had heard about Jesus was true, and if I refused to take that step of faith I would be living a lie for the rest of my life.

Darkness had fallen and the arc lights had come on. Walking across the sodden grass to the platform area I had the sense of something tremendous happening.

A lady came up to me. Felt hat pulled down, glasses, a bun, flat shoes and old enough to be my mother. My picture of a Christian.

But she was sweet. She asked me about myself. I didn't tell her I was Jewish because I was afraid she would say this wasn't for me, and tell me to go to a synagogue. She asked me if I'd like to go to church and I was appalled.

I went home more dejected and confused than ever, feeling I had done a terrible thing. Had I betrayed my Jewish heritage for a myth, a dream? I wanted Jesus, but did he want me?

She wrote to me very quickly. Her letter said she was pleased I had given my life to the Lord. I didn't understand her phraseology.

I read Billy Graham's book *Peace With God*. What an incredible book! The first words in it rang a bell with me: 'You started on the great quest the moment you were born.'

My new friend, whose name was Mary, invited me to her home where I talked and cried and she listened sympathetically. It turned out that she and her daughter had been converted at Harringay only the year before. I was astonished. She seemed to have such a deep personal knowledge of God—much better than mine, and I was supposed to be one of God's chosen people.

Eventually I met Mary's daughter, like me a secretary in the West End. She took me to a lunch hour service at All Souls, Langham Place. A young curate, John Collins, was preaching and it was just the same sort of simple, compelling message I had heard at Wembley. At the end I went up and told him I had committed my life to Christ but hadn't got linked with a church yet.

He beamed at me: 'In that case you couldn't do better than stay with us for a few weeks.'

Twenty-eight years later I am still there.

I joined a weekly Bible class led by Frances Whitehead, secretary to John Stott, the Rector. They called it a Nursery Class. It took me a long time to get it together, still having a foot in the old life of dancing and parties. Very slowly, as I read the New Testament and began to pray, and learn with other new Christians, Jesus became real and precious and wonderful and more desirable than anything or anybody in the world. It happened slowly because there were still places in my life where I wanted to do things my way. Soon I started going to Sunday services.

The sense of assurance came very dramatically, the following spring. I had been at a weekend house party for business people and it was my first experience of the kind of wholesome fun and Christian fellowship that wraps you round with love. On the coach coming back we were singing hymns, and when they dropped me at the end of my road the hymns stayed with me. I walked, singing. Suddenly I thought, 'Oh, it's all real and true.' The burden had lifted.

That summer I was baptized. Richard Bowdler prepared me and advised me that I should tell my parents and my ex-husband. I was aghast.

He said, 'You've got to come out in the open and tell the people who are nearest to you. There's no such thing as a secret disciple.'

So I rang my mother and told her I was going to be baptized. I said, 'I think I've been looking for God all my life, and now I've found him.'

'Well, I think I can understand that,' she responded, 'but why did you have to find him *this* way?'

Like a flash of light the answer came to me, 'Jesus said,

''I am the way, the truth and the life. No one comes to the Father except by me.'' So you see, there *isn't* any other way.'

She was stunned. 'Well, you must do what you think is right.'

I got strips torn off me afterwards by my brother and sister for upsetting my mother. I knew what it was about: my parents thought I was going to hate them. Jews always feel that about Christians and it's easy to see why when you think of the terrible history of anti-Semitism. But they soon realized that I didn't hate them. I went to see them every week from then on.

There were lots of opportunities to talk to Mother and Father in the next fourteen years before they died. They came quite a long way towards understanding my new faith in God. Mother had always been a great quoter of familiar bits like 'Silver and gold have I none...' without knowing who said it. That would give me an opportunity to read her the verse in context. She was quite open—just afraid of the unknown. She did come once to a service at All Souls, and always liked meeting my Christian friends.

My brother, however, was very up in arms:

'I'm born a Jew, I'll die a Jew. I say my prayers every night.'

When I told Mac I had committed my life to Christ and was going to be baptized as a Christian, a nice look came into his eyes, and he said 'I'm very glad for you.'

After that we got quite friendly on my visits to collect Malcolm. He married again and had another boy, which was good for Malcolm.

I attended the All Souls training school which prepared lay people for all kinds of work, like Sunday School teaching, house-to-house visiting and evangelism. I read every Christian book I could lay hands on, talked to strangers on buses and trains about Jesus, gave my testimony at lots of meetings (even in the street!) and went visiting in the parish with a friend.

We once called on Lew Grade. He opened the door, smoking a big cigar, and when we introduced ourselves as visitors from All Souls Church, he said 'I'm Jewish.'

'Delighted to meet you—so am I,' I replied. He looked quite taken aback. I had a few minutes' talk with him about Jesus the Messiah, while he stood there politely and listened, before firmly closing the door!

It was this kind of experience—calling 'cold' on people and sharing my faith with them—that helped me survive when I changed my job in 1964 to become a sales representative with Sun Life of Canada.

I was finding secretarial work very unfulfilling, and longing for something involving more personal contact, when I met John Smith, a dynamic Christian with Sun Life. He persuaded me that the job was tailor-made for me, and I joined his unit—made up almost entirely of Christians whom he had recruited and trained personally. I think it must be one of the hardest jobs anyone could do—especially a woman—but I'll always be glad I did it.

In 1965 John Stott, Rector of All Souls, astounded me by asking if I would take on the leadership of a Beginners' Group. I felt totally inadequate; nevertheless, having been in one myself, I appreciated the enormous value of this weekly Bible study for new Christians, and decided to say yes. I'm still with it.

We have people from varying backgrounds and age groups, with a whole range of problems. Often they are running away or searching for something. Or they are involved in the occult, drugs, Eastern religions, and are often living with somebody. Their lives have been messed up in one way or another, and they are bruised and hurting.

Because of this I felt the need for further training in

understanding people, and helping them in some of these areas, so I joined Care and Counsel, a Christian organization set up for that purpose. I also took a course at the Westminster Pastoral Foundation. What I've learned chiefly is how to listen—which is not as easy as it sounds, especially for the enthusiastic Christian who knows his Bible, has a text all ready, and can hardly wait to quote it. Properly understood, counselling involves creating a space into which the troubled soul can overspill, listening carefully and non-judgementally, then perhaps holding up a 'mirror', so he can see himself, his attitudes and behaviour a little more clearly. Only then is it possible to move on to something more positive and constructive.

As I grew more mature as a Christian and began to experience the peace which Jesus brought to my life, it made a lot of difference to my outings with Malcolm. When he was nine I took him to a CSSM beach mission at Felpham, and he told me he'd asked the Lord Jesus into his heart. I was overjoyed, and took him home with his little Scripture Union Bible reading notes. I told his father, and asked if he would help him read the Bible daily. I got a very cold reception, which I don't like to think about now, because Jesus spoke some very strong words against those who put a stumbling-block in the way of little children.

After that I took him to All Souls whenever I could, and talked often with him about what being a Christian meant. When I can, I always chat with him about it now, trying not to be too heavy.

He married a Roman Catholic girl, who goes to mass every Sunday, though he does not attend church. I am glad that his two children are being given an opportunity to learn about Jesus in their infancy, and I pray that they will grow up to know and love him.

It was at All Souls in 1983 that I met a staff member of Campus Crusade for Christ, an interdenominational

Christian movement that began in 1951 at the University of California, Los Angeles. About 250 students committed their lives to Christ during that first academic year, and the work spread rapidly, not only in the United States, but worldwide, until today there are around 10,000 full-time staff, working in 150 nations.

In 1967 a team of American staff responded to a call to begin a ministry in Britain. Since then, God has called many British people to join the staff, and currently there are over sixty working, not only among university students, but also in other areas, co-ordinated through the national headquarters at Reading.

The girl I met was one of a team involved in pioneering a new work among business and professional people in London. She invited me to join her on a survey being conducted among women in positions of influence, television newscasters, journalists, lawyers and business executives. This involved obtaining a personal interview, using a questionnaire to discover what part, if any, Christian faith played in the lives of the women we interviewed. I enjoyed this tremendously, and was thrilled at some of the opportunities we had for sharing our faith. Some of the women were willing to meet again for further talk.

The survey and interviews form one prong of the ministry. Another is the encouragement of Christians, not only to stand firm under all the pressures of the business and professional world, but to witness effectively. The more I learned about Campus Crusade's ministry among business and professional people, the more I sensed this was God's way ahead for me. My background, training and experience all equipped me for the job, and everything seemed to slot in perfectly with my ongoing work at All Souls.

Every few weeks we arrange an evangelistic supper party. In this friendly and informal atmosphere guests hear a short talk by an invited speaker on some relevant aspect of the Christian gospel, and have opportunity to talk with others present (often far into the night!). There are always some wanting to find out more, and we invite these to examine the claims of Christ in a weekly Bible-study arranged to run for about six weeks. One important aspect of these supper parties is that each guest has been brought by a Christian friend, who can keep contact in a natural and non-threatening way. We regularly see people come to a real commitment to Christ, and where there was one solitary Christian in an office, this has multiplied to two or three, growing and witnessing together, and reaching others.

The financial implications of exchanging a lucrative career selling life assurance for a job with no pay were somewhat daunting! Campus Crusade staff are supported entirely by personal friends who want to be involved a hundred per cent in our work of reaching people for Christ, and are anxious to give and pray to this end. I have been amazed and humbled at the interest and generous response of many. Their reactions were a confirmation that I was on track.

I sometimes wonder what would have happened to me if I had left Wembley that night, having rejected Christ's offer of new life. Who can say? I only know that that offer is for real. The God-shaped vacuum has been filled by its rightful occupant, and with him in control I have security, peace and purpose—none of which I knew before. Without doubt I would have continued rushing up one blind alley after another, trying to fill my life with all sorts of things or people which couldn't fit my need, and becoming more and more desperate and bitter. I would have made another disastrous marriage, because all my values were false and my needs were too great for anyone to meet.

Even after that night at Wembley it was very hard for me to accept singleness and, as I prayed and struggled, I longed to be able to add a 'lived happily ever after' line. Looking back now I think it is so good to be able to testify that the Christian life is not a bed of roses, nor an insurance policy against pain, sickness or heartache—but it is good news nonetheless.

We are asked to believe the good news, not because it will make us feel better, or provide those things which we equate with happiness, or give us a trouble-free life, but because it is true.

And if it is true that God loved me enough to send his Son Jesus Christ to die for me, then it is indeed worth spending my life sharing the news with a world that is dying for lack of love.

*'There was a contender for the welterweight title called Billy Graham—not quite in the same class as Sugar Ray Robinson . . .'*

# 4

# A Boxer Called Billy

When Fred Jinks was called up for army service at the age of 18 in 1944, his father told him, 'Use your loaf!' If he kept out of trouble, he would be OK. Fred took his advice. So when, during his primary military training in Newcastle the chaplain came round and asked if anyone wanted to be confirmed, Fred 'used his loaf' and volunteered. (The fact that this got him out of evening duties was pure coincidence...) But the confirmation classes were boring, so he gave them up.

Once the training course finished, he was posted to Whitby, where he was horrified to see that he was on the chaplain's list at the new camp. He stopped that straight away—he wasn't going to hob-nob with the chaplains, who were officers, from the wrong side of the street.

One of the padres there gave religion a bad name. He called all the young recruits together for a bit of a chat. He told them that he'd have to go back to tea and cakes with ladies after the war. He asked them if they knew any good dirty jokes. Fred and the lads were disgusted at this. Padres were allowed to be boring, but not dirty-minded or foul-mouthed. The meeting soon broke up.

But one soldier did impress Fred. In the dining-room, filled with men in full battle-dress, sat one soldier who bowed his head before eating. 'Talk about angel faces,' thought Fred, who had guessed what he was doing. He admired his courage, and the incident stuck in his mind. It became one of the pieces in the jigsaw that slowly built up to reveal that there was someone out there called God.

His training finally over, Fred was posted to Germany, and then to Egypt, where he acted as a driver in the 71st Anti-tank Regiment. The army gave him plenty of sport, and good friendship, but he was glad to see the back of it when, twenty-two months later, he secured an early discharge.

He returned to England, to the village of Wormley, in Hertfordshire. There he met a young Swiss woman called Marta Hess. Marta was a cook general at the Manor House, which was run by a Mrs Rhys Jones. Marta came from Schaffhausen, set on a hill above the River Rhine. She had answered an advertisement in her local paper to work in England—a country that she had always wanted to visit as she had a keen sense of adventure.

But England in 1947 was not all excitement. London struck Marta as being a very grey, bleak sort of place. The houses, walls, cars—even the people—all looked very dull. Smoke belched out of all the chimneys, and the air felt wet and gritty. To crown it all, the English ate their food out of tins…

Wormley was different—especially after she met Fred. Every evening the two of them would take Nevy, the dachshund, out for a walk. Mrs Rhys Jones invited Fred to the Manor House to size him up, and gave him her seal of approval. Fred and Marta continued to see each other for over two years, but then Marta's mother demanded that she return home. Marta obeyed—but she couldn't forget Fred.

The Jinks family also got together again, in London. Fred's parents found a house in Bow, in the East End, and Fred joined them. He soon found work, as a temporary cleaner, at the offices of *The Times*.

The paper operated a closed shop, which meant that no one could work there permanently without a ticket from the trade union, NATSOPA. But Fred got on well with the local 'chapel', and after a year as a temporary, he was voted in—a union man at last. Then the engineer–storekeeper, Tom Shirley, died rather suddenly. Fred got his job at a salary of £6.10s a week, which was quite enough to live on in those days.

Fred was now in a responsible position. He was in charge of thirty tons of materials for every department, from the general office supplies to the white spirit for cleaning down the machines. He went into all the different departments of the big, throbbing newspaper, and met everyone from the managers downwards.

He was also a keen sportsman. He enjoyed playing football after work, and swimming, running and rowing with The Times Amateur Athletic Association. One of his triumphs was to score a hat-trick of goals for *The Times* in a NATSOPA shield final against Odhams, making the score 4–1.

Life held almost everything his heart could desire at 28. He had a number of girlfriends, and even got engaged once, although later it was called off. He even thought of Marta—now and again. But March 1, 1954 changed everything...

One of Fred's football team mates, Lionel Phillips from editorial, dropped round after work, before going on to what he called a 'Billy Graham meeting' over in the big sports stadium at Harringay. Fred had no idea what on earth he was talking about, but as he had nothing better to do he decided to go along with him.

Fred was curious. Big posters shouting out the name 'Billy Graham' suggested only one thing to him: that there was a contender for the welterweight title called Billy Graham—not quite in the same class as Sugar Ray Robinson. Inside the arena it looked exactly as if a world boxing contest was about to take place, except that people filled the seats where the ring should have been, and there was a platform down at the front. Powerful lights beamed down, and there were pressmen taking down the words and popping flashbulbs.

Billy Graham told a story about a time he had flown over the Rocky Mountains, when everything became enveloped with snow. The radio had given out, and the navigator had lost contact with the ground.

'Some of you,' Billy told the audience, 'are going round and round aimlessly in your lives because you have lost contact with God.' He went on to say how the communication had been broken because of sin, but that Jesus Christ was the mediator between God and man and had restored the link. Much to his surprise, Fred found himself agreeing with everything he said.

Billy Graham then asked those who wanted to commit their lives to Christ to come forward. Fred sat in amazement as he watched the human tide flow down to the front from all over the building. Finally he could stand it no longer, and got up to go forward.

He had to go out of one door and into another to get to the front. The attendant held the door into the arena half open and asked him if he was coming in. Fred was now standing near the exit out of the stadium into the night. He knew he could slip out, go home and never come back. But it was dark and snowing outside—and the door into the arena was alight and welcoming. He went through.

A young man came up and ushered him into the counselling area, and asked Fred if he knew what he had done.

What, indeed, had he done, he thought. He knew that he had committed himself, while Billy was speaking, and told the man so. The counsellor went over the ground with him, just to make sure, and then asked if he had any problems. Fred had: he was worried about how he would tell his mates the next day that he had become a Christian.

'Let's pray about it,' suggested the young man. Then he said to Fred, 'You pray.' So Fred, who had never willingly been to church in his life, and who had refused to be confirmed, knelt with the counsellor, and talked to God as a friend, introduced himself and his problem, thanked him for the new world just opened to him through Jesus who had borne away his sin, and rose feeling himself accepted. Fred Jinks had been born again.

As he walked home he did not feel alone. He had a strong warmth in his heart, a glow in the chilly night. He felt good—alive! Later he was to identify closely with the reaction of the two on the road to Emmaus in Luke 24: 'Did not our hearts burn with us when he talked with us by the way?'

Back home in Islington he lost no time in telling his sister that he had been converted. He was relieved that he had shared his new faith with someone.

Next day, though, it wasn't quite so easy. The morning's papers were full of the previous night's happenings at Harringay, with photographs of people streaming out. Suppose his face was in there? Fred suddenly thought. He felt sick at the very idea. To make matters worse, the man next to him in the bus queue got very agitated. 'Look at this lot,' he complained to Fred, 'Haven't they got any English ministers or priests who could do this? Why did they have to import Americans?' Fred, who could usually put the world to rights with complete self-confidence, didn't take the bait. He was too busy poring over every picture he could see.

Up in The Times canteen over tea, toast and the news-papers, the conversation again turned to American evangelists. Fred said nothing, too scared to speak. He wasn't known for keeping quiet, and one of the men soon noticed that he was not his usual self. 'Don't tell me you went to Harringay last night, Fred?' he asked in disbelief.

This was it. He would *have* to speak. 'Yes I did,' replied Fred.

There was a deathly silence as this sunk in. 'Don't tell me,' another man chipped in, 'that you went out to the *front*?'

'Yes,' said Fred, 'I did.' He was relieved that he had managed to pass the test and stand up for his faith, just like the soldier he had seen all those years ago saying his grace in the mess hall.

News of his conversion spread swiftly round the build-ing. People pulled his leg and expected he would soon 'snap out of it'. One man, who had known him a long time, asked him if he'd had a bang on the head. On another occasion as he was walking through the publishing department all the staff burst into a rousing chorus of 'Onward Christian Soldiers'. Fred simply grinned—to him it was a compliment, even if it was a backhanded one.

He was avalanched with questions. He hadn't a Bible or a church behind him, but he always held his own. He had read the gospel according to John that had been given to him at Harringay, and remembered bits of Billy Graham's sermon. He still had the warm glow, but was now wonder-ing what to do next.

He decided to look for a church. The first one he found was a Seventh Day Adventist. He wrote 'What can I do?' on a slip of paper and handed it in with his collection, but forgot to add his address. He then went to an evening service in an Anglican church, but that didn't do much for him either.

At this point Fred was rescued by Peter Collins of the Circulation Department, who invited him to his church, Westminster Chapel, in the centre of London near Buckingham Palace. Peter took him to a Friday evening Bible study. The preacher was, as usual, the great Bible teacher, Dr Martyn Lloyd-Jones, known in Christian circles as 'The Doctor'. Dr Lloyd-Jones was working through a series of sermons on the key doctrines of the Christian faith.

Peter wondered what Fred would make of it all, but he needn't have worried. When the sermon finished, Fred said, 'That was really interesting—that man has got something to teach me.'

At the end of the evening, Peter Collins introduced Fred to Dr Lloyd-Jones. The Doctor listened carefully to everything Fred had to say and when he had finished, he said, 'Mr Jinks, my door is always open to you—always regard me as your friend and pastor.'

Dr Lloyd-Jones prayed and then Peter and Fred left the vestry. Within a short time Fred had joined the mid-week Bible class, and felt fully at home at the Chapel. It wasn't long before he was giving his testimony at the Bible study, and one of his many new friends provided him with a Bible of his own. He was made a sidesman, and became a much-loved member of the church community.

His growing confidence showed itself at work, where he was now able to give reasons for his beliefs. Some of his former friends decided that there was something odd about him, and left him alone. But Fred wasn't bothered. Why should he be ashamed of being saved by the Lord Jesus Christ? he thought.

One day he told one of his work-mates, who reckoned himself an expert on religion, that he needed to be born again. Fred really laid it on thick. That was what Billy

Graham had said—now he would tell people too. He told another man: 'What a wonderful thing when you can go to a Person and he changes you and makes you born again—a "new creation".'

Meanwhile, back in Schaffhausen, Marta had never stopped thinking about Fred. One day she heard that he was in town, visiting another girl, called Annemarie, whom he had known in Wormley. She felt hurt that he hadn't visited her, but she was too proud to go and find him herself. No, she thought, the man should make the first move.

At last her mother, taking pity on her, arranged for them to meet outside the cinema. It had been five years... but it was as if they had never parted.

Fred went home, but promised to write to her every day. And he kept his word. He wrote a dozen cards at a time, and posted one a day. Every day the postman toiled all the way up the hill to Marta's home with a letter or a card.

But in his heart of hearts he felt uneasy about their relationship. He knew that Marta, for all her charms, was not born again in the way Billy Graham used the words. He knew that the Bible said that a Christian should not be married ('unequally yoked') to an unbeliever, and didn't know what to do about the situation.

His friends told him that Marta was a long way off, and all he had to do was to say 'no' and that would be the end of the matter. But he found he couldn't be that cold-blooded where his feelings were involved. Finally he decided to speak to the Doctor, quite prepared to do whatever he suggested.

Dr Lloyd-Jones knew that Marta, although not a born again Christian, was always willing to listen to the claims of the gospel. His advice, gravely considered, was direct: 'Go ahead and marry her... and convert her.'

Glad and relieved, Fred went ahead. And no man could have said that Fred didn't try to 'convert' his Swiss miss. He also wanted her to know exactly what she would be taking on in marrying him.

His letters were full of religion, church meetings and the Sunday school. In the end Marta lost her temper; she decided that if his next letter was one of his long religious sermons, she would give him up!

Next day she waited anxiously as the postman climbed up the hill. Yes, there was a letter. Hardly daring to breathe, she opened it...the tears came. It was what a real love letter ought to be. It was not 'religious' at all—just 'God bless you, Fred' at the end.

Frau Hess had never hidden the fact that she disapproved of Fred for her daughter. He had once spent a holiday with them and overstayed his leave, losing his lodgings and job as a result. However, this stream of correspondence from England was getting on her nerves. She ordered Marta to marry Fred or stop dithering.

Until that moment, Marta had allowed her mother to plan her life, but now a new purpose and sense of dignity took hold of her. She went to town, bought a ticket for Fred to come over for Christmas and told him that they were getting engaged. Fred was startled, but didn't object.

He was due to arrive at 5 pm on Christmas Eve. So Marta had to smile sweetly at the jeweller in order to persuade him to keep the shop open so that Fred could buy the ring. While Fred was still busy studying the tray, Marta chose a plain gold band for Fred's finger, and paid for it. Fred remained indecisive—was he having second thoughts? Marta wondered. But eventually all was made clear. A Swiss girl did not expect a jewelled engagement ring. She would wear a plain gold band on her right hand until the wedding ceremony, and thereafter wear it on her left hand.

Greater difficulties lay ahead—the young couple had nowhere to live. Fred, though, took comfort from a verse from Scripture: 'Seek ye first the Kingdom of God and his righteousness, and all these things shall be added unto you.'

Shortly after this, Uncle Jim and Aunt Sue in Poplar, in the East End, provided the answer by offering the newly-weds their own big bedroom and front room.

The wedding finally took place on June 4th 1955 at the Zwingli Munster Kapelle in Schaffhausen. They spent their wedding night in Marta's own room at home, and Fred knelt by the bed and prayed for his wife's conversion. He couldn't help feeling hurt when she laughed.

Back in London the young couple made the best of their two rooms, before moving on to a flat of their own, where two of their four children were born.

Nine months after the wedding, Fred's prayer was answered. Marta heard a sermon of Dr Lloyd-Jones that changed her life. He mentioned two mountains that a traveller wanted to cross. There was only one way to do it, he said—a bridge. To a girl like Marta brought up in the mountains, the picture came alive.

She suddenly realized that what she really needed was someone to reconcile her to God. It was, she said later, like a light switching on—you don't need to know how electricity works for the light to come on. She now saw things clearly that had until recently been a mystery—she was born again, just as Fred had been in Harringay.

In August 1960 Fred was voted player of the year by The Times football club. But it was the end of a chapter. In 1960 Westminster Chapel needed a verger, and solid, reliable Fred was given the job. The Chapel, often nick-named the Cathedral of the free church movement, with its galleries, 2,300 seats, and huge pulpit, sees not only its own 2,000 regulars coming Sunday by Sunday, but also thousands of visitors throughout the year.

Fred found himself—as he still does today—with numerous housekeeping tasks behind the scenes to keep services running smoothly and punctually. He is truly a 'doorkeeper in the house of the Lord'—and the door always has well-oiled hinges!

Fred, always on the spot, is often the first call when someone wants advice. 'Go back to your church and wait till God tells you to leave,' he once advised a troubled visitor, wanting to know whether or not to change denomination. It was the sort of reply the Doctor would have given. In all this, Marta is a faithful ally—her German, French and Italian are useful with the many foreign visitors that pass through, and her sound common-sense is well known for solving many of the problems that arise in a busy place such as the Chapel.

After twenty-three years of hearing some of the greatest preachers of our time at Westminster Chapel, Fred can recite an impressive list of memorable men. Two stand out among the giants.

The first is Pastor Niemöller, the man whose courageous stand against Hitler cost him many years in a concentration camp. The second is Billy Graham, who preached at mid-week meetings over the years. Each time it was Fred's job to show the men to the preacher's vestry, and then conduct them to the pulpit. Somehow, though, Fred never got round to telling Billy Graham that he was converted at Harringay. 'I think,' says Fred, 'that is what people call English reserve!'

His association with Martyn Lloyd-Jones has left Fred with many personal memories of the man behind the ministry, and an awareness that he too had a part in great events.

'No one,' Fred fondly recalls, 'will know what a wonderful atmosphere there was in the services conducted by the Doctor unless they had experienced the blessings themselves, especially his prayers. His preaching appealed to a great many intellectual and gifted people, but most ordinary people got just as much from them.' One thing that always intrigued Fred was that foreigners, with limited English vocabulary, could follow his expositions.

The Doctor retired from the Chapel in 1968, and his successor is Dr R. T. Kendall. Like the Doctor, he holds evangelistic services on Sunday evenings, and has begun a scheme called Pilot Lights.

Every Saturday morning a group hold a prayer meeting, then for two hours go out on to the streets to give away tracts, and invite people to the Sunday services. Many people have been converted as a result.

The Chapel is soldiering on into the 1980s, with new life flowing in as ever. And in the middle of it all, ready for anything, is Fred Jinks, one of the best known vergers of any church, anywhere. Fred's life has certainly changed since the night he went to see 'a boxer called Billy'!

*'Men and women cannot live without hope. If we want to survive we must have a basis for hope'* (Billy Graham).*

# 5

## *Nowhere Men*

Bob Funnell would dearly like to forget his childhood, but he finds he cannot. One bleak memory is of something his mother said as he came through the door of their Dagenham house with his father, just back from evacuation.

'What have you brought him home here for? I don't want him,' she said to his father.

Young Bob trembled. Without being able to articulate it, he felt as if he were poised on the edge of nowhere, about to fall. Home but not at home. These words were to colour the whole of his life.

There were seven children in the Funnell household. Dad was a tool-maker. Mother—well, she was a church-goer, but her religion was like a Sunday dress, not for everyday. She kept her family short of love—Bob especially.

He was a gangly, short-sighted lad, who was never the centre of attention. He had a few friends at the secondary modern school but life, even at 12 or 13, had taught him to

*Decision*, November 1982.

be wary of trusting anyone too much. Like a plant stunted for sunshine so he was thwarted and weakened by a lack of love and care.

The only bit of happiness in that home came to Bob from Doris, his eldest sister who had, somehow, truly found Christ as Saviour at the Anglican church they attended on their mother's insistence. Whereas Bob had passed through Sunday school and Sunday services without a ripple, Doris had plunged in and found the truth and grasped it, like a lifebelt.

She tackled her young brother: 'Bob, give your heart to Jesus... he'll help you through.'

He could see it was working for her but he wouldn't give in on principle. Doris, though, was a real blessing. His senior by several years, she stuck up for him and mothered him.

After Doris, Bob loved his bicycle best. He got his first decent one at 15 when he started work as a trainee mechanic in a cycle factory. He bought the frame and parts and put it together himself. Later he had his own business, mending bikes and making them up. He loved them and spent hours out in the shed at the back of the house, repairing, polishing, and improving his own and other people's machines.

At about this time he stopped going to church and escaped into the countryside on Sundays, joining the Cyclists Touring Club. Not that he always needed company. With a fishpaste sandwich and a bottle of lemonade in his saddlebag he was self-sufficient, a free-wheeling spirit on the open roads. Summer lay warm and sweet on the fields; villages hid at the ends of flowery lanes. The Bible given him by Doris stayed buried in the depths of the cupboard, but the book of creation opened to him as he sped homewards in the dusk, keeping company with the bats and owls that swooped over hedges and barns and church towers and tall elms.

Holidays found him touring farther afield, sleeping in youth hostels. In Wales he challenged, with puny strength, the mountains' grand designs. Always he had that sense of a presence in nature, though he wasn't ready to name it.

Once on the bridge at Abridge, Essex, he sat on his bike watching a man give out tracts. It was November, and the cold winds were sweeping the dying leaves into the hedges. The few people about were hurrying home to a hot lunch. Bob shivered suddenly and wondered if the future held anything more for him than this—an endless tour, with no place to call 'home'.

At that moment the tract distributor came over and offered him a leaflet. But Bob brushed him off: 'I used to go to church,' he said dismissively.

'It's not church you need...it's Jesus,' said the man, pressing the tract on him. Bob afterwards tore up the tract and let the pieces blow away on the wind. The man's words stayed with him, though.

'Coming to hear Billy Graham, Bob? Oh, go on, you must!' Bob felt Doris was being a real pain in the neck over the Harringay meetings. Still, by all accounts they sounded quite exciting, he thought, if you liked that sort of thing. He was 20 now, and he could choose his own way in life. He chose to please Doris.

'Oh, all right. I'll go just once if it'll stop your nagging,' he said, without rancour. They understood each other.

Sitting jammed in the middle of a row between Doris and his mother he was careful to let his expression betray no emotion.

It was George Beverley Shea, the gospel singer, who really reached his heart. 'He's got the whole world in his hands' sang the big man, and it came home to Bob, like a shaft of purest light, that someone cared after all. He might be insignificant to the world but someone had put the price of his own life on him. He wanted to respond to that gift but his mother was sitting there, with an 'I'm-all-right-Jack' face, and he decided he would not give her the satisfaction of seeing him go for counselling.

A week later, however, he went back to Harringay alone, to do what he had to do. He had been thinking of little else all week. When the appeal came he was out at the front like a shot. Doris was delighted.

'I felt what he was saying was right,' he told his delighted sister, later.

The Sunday cycling continued but a hunger and thirst for God's way began to make itself felt. First he took to coming back early to get to church in the evening, and then the Sunday jaunts stopped completely, the Bible came permanently out of the cupboard and he learned to pray. One remarkable answer to prayer was that he studied for and passed an O-level in English, externally. He was changing, with God's help.

One day he took a long, hard look at himself and the people around him. Bob realized his mother's religion was nothing more than a habit formed in childhood when her father was in 'trade'. Tradesmen went to church then because it was good for business—like voting Conservative. He saw his sister as the good angel of the home. Her prayers, he was convinced, had brought him through. He saw his father, once kindly and patient with him, growing sour.

Bob's sudden adoption of religion had opened a great divide at home, and the tensions there were aggravated by the fact that Dad seemed to be finding solace elsewhere. Matters came to a head when Bob made the mistake of remonstrating, and in a terrible scene his father told him and Doris, in words Bob would rather not recall, to 'go and not come back'.

They were on the streets, homeless. They went into lodgings: Bob to North London and then back to Dagenham; Doris went to Hornchurch. She almost went on bended knee at the council offices to find them a home, but it was no use.

In the end their vicar put in a word and they got a rundown flat in an old almshouse. It had an outside toilet, a canvas bath, weeping walls and mice in the cellar. Later it was condemned and pulled down. It was home for nine years while they waited for a council house. They had been to rock bottom. The only way out was up.

Bob often tried to talk to the vicar about their situation, but it was hopeless. He was a good man and a sound gospel preacher, but had little understanding of problems of that order of magnitude. Bob, who had been a misfit at home, now began to feel a misfit at church.

Still, he lent a hand wherever he could. He found he had a knack for getting on with the awkward ones—the ones who dropped in out of the rain at evening service and sat at the back waiting for the price of a cup of tea. It was always left to Bob to solve the problem of what to do.

'Because they're awkward, it doesn't mean they shouldn't be shown love,' he told the people who complained about the unwelcome visitors. Bob understood only too well what it was like to feel unwanted.

The Keswick meetings in Dagenham, to which members of all the churches came, held a surprise for him one year: he suddenly felt God was calling him to be a missionary. A young fellow from the Philippines had been speaking and at the end three young people stood to declare their willingness to go wherever God should lead them. Bob just sat there, lacking the courage to declare himself.

Nevertheless, the call stood. It shone with purpose. He was wanted. But where? Of one thing he was sure, he lacked the stamina to be a C. T. Studd and go abroad.

It was soon after this that Bob became friendly with a London City missionary who lived and worked locally. Whatever it took to be godly Mr Walter Wallace certainly had. The Queen must have thought so too, because she gave him the traditional Maundy money one year.

Bob became more and more interested in Mr Wallace's work and began to ask questions.

'If you want to be a City missionary you've got to know your Bible. You need a thorough working knowledge. So go home and study it and do a lot of practical work,' was Mr Wallace's advice.

Bob did just that. Sunday school teaching, youth work, visiting—he redoubled his efforts. At home he studied Bible courses, lacking the money to go to college. Everything was geared to his goal.

In 1960 he applied to the London City Mission. He couldn't understand why God wanted him but his call was real enough. It was mysterious, sovereign. He knew that his life was no longer his own, because God, in his infinite wisdom, had stooped down to pick him for a piece of work in his vineyard. It gave life a meaning and a dignity never before realized.

However, Bob found it wasn't so easy to get this over to the selection board. 'Do you have a scripture verse to back up your call?' they asked.

'Yes,' replied Bob, 'Isaiah 6:8—"Here am I send me."'

A barrage of questions followed. What Christian work have you done? Do you smoke or drink? Are you married? What Bible study courses have you taken? What kind of work would you like to do within the Mission?

He knew the answer to the last question immediately: he wanted to work amongst the down and outs, the homeless; he was supremely well qualified.

So Bob was accepted and began his training. He enjoyed the work, but sometimes felt lonely and wished he had a wife. 'It's not in man to stick to God's work year in, year out, alone, is it? I only do it because Someone up there has his hand on me,' he told his friends, Eddy and Irene Stride.

One day, in desperation, he joined a Christian pen pal club and, after a discreet interview, had received the address of someone called Hazel in Birmingham.

Nervously, Bob took the coach to Birmingham to meet Hazel and her parents. She was about his age, in her mid-thirties, yet seemed younger. She was an only and cherished child of a Christian home—a home where love ruled. Bob liked Hazel immediately and warmed at once to her mother. However, Hazel's mother was a little more cautious about Bob. His appearance did not suggest he could support himself, let alone her daughter.

Initially, Hazel felt somewhat wary of Bob. She had gone on to the pen-pal list because she was lonely and most of her friends were married. And now, after three years of waiting and feeling at a dead end, this stranger had sprung out of the blue. They peered at each other— and Hazel wasn't too sure about what she saw. He was a lonely bachelor, working among down and outs—and he looked the part. Eventually, she confided to her mother: 'I wish he'd go. I'll be glad when it's Monday morning.'

But by Monday the strain had worn off and they both started to feel that God really was using this unusual way of answering the desire of both their hearts.

One small detail came as a surprising confirmation. Hazel had also been converted under Billy Graham's ministry—as long ago as 1947, when the young Youth for Christ evangelist came to Birmingham. She was 15 and just at the age to rebel against parents who seemed not to know what fun was to be had out in the world.

Sitting next to her parents at the meeting she did not outwardly respond yet felt troubled. She remembered how she had once answered an evangelist's question 'Are you saved?' with a lie. That 'yes' stuck in her memory, accusingly. So after the meeting she knelt by her bed and gave her life to Jesus for his purpose—and her teenage rebellion sank without trace.

Three months after their first encounter Bob and Hazel became engaged. They were old enough to know that they had been kept for each other. There was no point, as Bob said, in 'dragging it out'.

Hazel's church friends were, however, concerned for her welfare: 'You've never been anywhere on your own! Fancy you going to London! You're making the biggest mistake,' they warned.

'No, I'm not. I've got peace of mind,' said the once-timid Hazel. But, just to make sure, on their engagement weekend, Bob took Hazel down to London for a few days to stay with his sister and to see whether his work among the down and outs in the grubbier corners of Bethnal Green and Bow would put her off. It didn't. She was quite sure that this was where she ought to be, with Bob.

The wedding took place at Bloomsbury FIEC Church, Birmingham on August 14th 1971. Hazel wore powder blue and the honeymoon was spent at Shanklin and Ventnor—places Bob had often explored in his lonely bachelor days. This time he did not take his bike.

With Hazel in London it was like going from rags to riches. First, Bob asked the Mission for a proper home, and got it. Secondly, he had a wife who was a true helpmeet. They found that the secret of harmonious living was to share Bible reading and prayer times. Bob had seen too many other rocky marriages to risk his own by leaving God out of the day.

Thirdly, Hazel was a willing helper with the Day Centre project, Bob's dream. He longed to help the drop-outs of society and it was like a dream fulfilled when the Mission appointed him to work among them. With Ricky Fawcett, a Geordie and a former boiler maker, he helped to start the first Mission Day Centre for down and outs in Bermondsey, in 1973. Ricky also worked among the gypsies and Bob undertook work among news-vendors.

Many a time Bob had wanted somewhere to invite a man off the streets for a bite and a hot drink. The need for warm clothing in winter also created a problem.

'Got a coat, Bob?' the drifters would ask in the street. Bob might have, but he couldn't carry it about with him. The Centre was the place to store and distribute the clothes that people generously gave for the purpose. Hazel took over the running of the kitchen at the Centre, and has run it ever since, with willing helpers, providing gallons of soup, rolls and tea twice a week, and a proper dinner at Christmas.

The Centre has since transferred to the Bethnal Green United Reformed Church. The hall is hardly Buckingham Palace, but the patrons don't seem to object. They are not a chatty bunch. Each man is wrapped in his own isolation. One of the men brings his dog for its saucer of milk. Another, with blunted fingers, roughs out a sentimental ditty on the old piano in the corner—his grandma, he told them once, used to play at church.

The men swallow the food and tea and listen to the Bible talk without showing interest or emotion. Bob and Ricky give out clothes and exchange a few words with individuals. It is often thankless work for which they see little result, but they press on. Bob is totally dedicated to his 'odd-bods'. It is his calling, which he can't get away from. He knows why:

'I could have been exactly the same as they are. I could have thought, "Nobody cares for me. Why should I care for myself?"

'Behind it all, some look like respectable people. They

get to be drop-outs through an unhappy home life... drink mainly. With some it could be war neurosis. Some are a bit backward. A lot had no real home to start with. Until recent times, the council couldn't care less about you if you were single and wouldn't house you. Those fellows who live in hostels have got no hope of a council place, or a proper home... no hope at all.

'An address is vital, or a receipt. Then the Social Security will give you "bed money" for your lodgings. If you haven't an address you don't get anything. They've got no check-up... you can see the Social Security's point of view.'

The missionaries don't pry. They take a man for what he is, come alongside and try to help where they can, treating him as an adult when he asks for clothes.

'Some places will ask them to hand in their dirty shirt, if they give out a clean one,' Bob says. 'We see why they do it, but we don't agree. We'll take a man at his word. Sometimes I'm a bit tight on shoes and coats. They have to put their name in the book for those.'

Bob finds his customers in the parks, demolition sites, along the Embankment, under the railway arches and in the stations. 'They keep moving round in a circle... London and farther afield. I met one of them in Birmingham.

'The men don't starve, because if you know where to look in London there is always free food to be had, thrown out by the hotels, if you are not too fussy.'

The men carry everything with them in plastic bags, and they throw stuff away when it gets dirty and turn up for replacements. In summer they often sleep rough, but in the main they go into the hostels in the winter.

His down and outs maintain slight contact with civilization, even if only for the sake of a shirt:

'I often say to the lads: "What bottle are you on?" They

know me well enough by now and will tell me. The worst cases take meths. Jake, it's called…a mixture of VP wine, methylated spirits and boot polish. Vile stuff.'

How does Bob measure the results of his life's work?

'It's not easy to quantify,' he replies. 'I've long accepted that my personal ministry is a warning one. I've got nobody's soul on my conscience. I've tried faithfully over the years to show them the way… be a link in the chain. People are always saying to me, "How many souls have you won? How many people have you led to the Lord?" Well I have led people to the Lord, but in the main one sows and another reaps.'

Bob's whole life and work is devoted to trying to help misfits put the jumbled puzzles of their lives together. Social measures are important and necessary, but can't change the basic problem—the nature of the man—as God can.

And so Bob has confidence in what he does, however discouraging it is at times. And he thanks God for Billy Graham:

'What I learned at Harringay was that somebody cared for me. It doesn't matter what the world thinks of me, God cares for me. What I am doing today is the result of that experience. I am passing on the truth that God cares for all the odd-bods, the misfits, and finds them a place in his kingdom, and can renew and reshape their lives.'

This caring love, which heals our past and all its memories, was shown to Bob recently. He had been telling a Christian family about the train set he never had as a child, but had always longed for. Months went by. Christmas came. He visited the family and to his surprise received a present. With a loving instinct the family had given him a train set. He, quite overwhelmed, learned in a new way that God heals the broken-hearted, and loves to write happy endings to their saddest stories.

*'You are not ready to live until you are ready to die'*
(Dr R. T. Kendall).*

# 6

## *'You Only Live Once!'*

It was January, 1946. A jeep was riding the pot-holed,
muddy road towards Maymyo from north-east Burma,
carrying Lieutenant John Lewis and his Gurkha driver
and bearer to the local HQ of 33 Corps Troop Engineers,
Indian Army.

John, at 21, was in charge of a detachment of Bengal
Sappers and Miners who were building Bailey bridges to
reopen roads cut to halt the Japanese advance during the
Burma campaign. The war was over, but pockets of
Japanese troops were still hiding in the jungle, and the
Indian Army was flushing them out.

The young lieutenant bent his head to light a cigarette,
so failed to see a heavily laden Burmese truck appear,
swinging drunkenly towards them on the twisting, axle-
breaking road. Within seconds, the driver had lost control
and rammed the side of the jeep.

By a miracle of timing another truck was on the scene,
full of British sergeants on reconnaissance. They gathered
up the accident victims and rushed them twenty miles to

*\*What Is Christianity?*, Westminster Tracts No. 1.

the field hospital.

Lieutenant Lewis had suspected ruptured kidneys and was passing blood. He needed transfusions and was unconscious for three days. The consultant surgeon flown in from Singapore to examine the young lieutenant looked grave as he gave his verdict: 'If this chap recovers, he'll be out of action for eighteen months.'

In sheer desperation John prayed. 'Oh God, please get me out of here and back to my bridges!' he pleaded. He had not prayed since childhood. He wondered if there really was a God to hear and help.

In just thirty days, to everyone's amazement, John walked out of the field hospital. He returned to his Bailey bridges without a backward thought.

When John returned to England, he decided to dedicate himself to studying for a BSc degree in Estate Management, and worked extremely hard towards this goal.

However, walking away from the final examination three years later, he was assailed by fear—and for the second time in his life he sent up an SOS: 'Get me through this, God. I'll be a better man if you do.' Empty words to a Father Christmas figure sitting on a fluffy white cloud.

He passed—of course—and life took off spectacularly. He worked hard, played hard, ran a fast car, and roared home from West End theatres and night clubs in the small hours, with a merry load of revellers—and then had to drag himself out of bed for work, short on sleep and short in temper.

By the age of 30 he was a chartered surveyor with a firm of valuers in the West End, living it up in the supertax bracket and with a fiancée, Julie. 'Life is good—you only live once', he told himself loud and often. He had money and pleasure and yet...a whisper inside would not be silenced: 'What's it all *for*?' More than once he felt drawn to those shining tracks as the London tube trains slid by.

There was no help from his family. Dad lived for a game of snooker and a pint with friends. His sister, Meg, who'd had the time of her life in the WRNS was, at 28, a sophisticated, fun-loving blonde, and very fed-up with Tadworth village life. She'd had a string of men friends, the latest of whom had turned out to be married. She was into her fourth job since demob—not even the round of parties could chase away the boredom.

Much to John's amazement, shortly after this Meg announced that she had given her life to Christ. Out of idle curiosity she had been with a friend to see the film *Oiltown USA*. Billy Graham's words, though, had really hit home and had forced Meg to look at her futile way of life.

John wasn't sure he liked this new meek creature who was helping their tired mother around the house, and claiming to be 'converted'. Meg had given up rushing around with her men friends and was attending a prayer meeting in Kingswood. Sundays she spent at church. John even suspected her of praying for him.

'Poor kid,' he thought. 'She's gone round the bend... gone to religion for consolation, intead of getting married.'

But Meg was soon on John's trail. Billy Graham was at Harringay and she wanted her brother to hear him.

'Not on your life,' John said. 'I don't want to hear some American telling us British people what to do. I'm not interested in all that mumbo-jumbo.'

Meg kept up the pressure, though, and when someone at the office who was a steward at the crusade, invited him along, John gave in.

So early in May he took Julie to Harringay stadium. Meg had arranged a coach party and it included their parents.

If John had half expected to see a few little old ladies in black rattling round an empty stadium he was in for a shock. It was crammed with more than 10,000 people, all looking extremely full of life. He had never heard such singing.

He and Julie sat smoking and laughing at everything, making it clear they were there for the show, and nothing else. Then a great big man got up to sing *He's got the whole world in his hands*.

Soft sort of man, singing hymns about God, thought John.

*He's got the tiny little baby in his hands*, sang Bev Shea. And yet, John had never seen such a look of love on any man's face in all his thirty years. Something magical took place in his own heart...softening, for he loved little children.

Then Billy Graham got up to speak. 'There are some people here tonight who couldn't care less about God,' he began.

'That's me,' thought John. Three things suddenly became crystal clear to him: that he had left God out of his life, though he owed some sort of allegiance to his Creator; that Jesus of Nazareth was God, not just the founder of a religion; and that he died on the cross for John Lewis.

When the appeal began a secret struggle raged. He was conscious of forty pairs of Tadworth eyes behind him. He had been out with some of their daughters and was known as a bright spark. He didn't want to look foolish, but there was an overwhelming compulsion.

John turned to Julie. 'Come with me?' But she shook her head.

'Well *I* must,' he said resolutely and went down, walking on air, a picture of a man who had at last found the answer to life's mystery.

As he stood at the front, a hand touched his shoulder. His father had taken courage from John's boldness and was coming from the no-man's-land of lost faith, where he had lived for almost forty years.

John's decision had one traumatic effect. Julie tried later to take the same step, but could not. Finally, she flung his ring back and walked out of his life for good.

Mrs Lewis, though, was still opposed to 'all this nonsense'. However, on the last night of the Harringay crusade, in spite of the fact that Meg had no tickets, she went with her daughter, partly because she 'liked the singing'.

There was a queue of people outside. Meg's hopes sank to zero. Suddenly, a boy ran up to her and, pushing two tickets into her hands, disappeared into the crowd. They were for seats right at the back. And so Mrs Lewis, with her arthritic knees, sat like the Rock of Gibraltar, comfortably secure from attack by any evangelist.

Then Billy said, 'I think there's somebody—the last member of the family perhaps—and you're sitting right up there and you haven't yet come to Christ.'

There was a creak of a seat and Mrs Lewis had gone—not walking, but running, to the counselling room, for fear (as she later said) of being too late!

Soon after this the family joined a local Evangelical Free Church in Tadworth, and John quickly became involved. He ran a businessmen's Bible study and training group; he counselled at Wembley; and he was commissioned as a lunch-hour worker at All Souls, Langham Place, where John Stott had a thriving outreach ministry.

At a meeting led by Stephen Olford some words rang in his heart and soul—*Only one life; 'twill soon be past; only what's done for Jesus will last.'*

He stood up to commit himself irrevocably, paying at last the vows he had made so lightly in those tarnished, selfish prayers of the past.

Bright young business men and women were flowing into London in search of career opportunities, in the post-war era. Several major churches organized lunch-hour services to attract them. It was here that John first met his future wife—a dedicated and charming young woman, Olga Code, who had organized a lunch-hour Bible discussion group at Church House, Westminster, attended by about 100 young people. He thought it a good idea and started several groups in other places.

John longed to become a full-time Christian worker, but his advisers counselled patience.

At Tadworth John tried unsuccessfully to get the church members out on house to house visiting. He told them:

'No one in all my 30-odd years ever talked to me about a personal Saviour. Surely we should be communicating with our neighbours?' It was the recurring theme of his life. But when he tried going round the houses with Sidney Perrin he felt awkward and people did not leap up to follow Christ as John had somehow supposed they would, once they had heard.

John and Olga were married on June 7th 1958, at Ross Road Hall, Wallington. Their three-bedroomed semi-detached house in Sanderstead quickly became a gathering point for young people from a newly built free church, Mitchley Hill Chapel, and in due course the house rang with the fun and laughter of two lovely daughters, Jane and Sally. Life was good. There was purpose and security in the centre of God's will.

There was an unsatisfied desire, though—they both wanted a son. Several miscarriages onwards, with Olga in her mid-thirties, the whole enterprise looked doubtful but the couple continued hoping and praying. To their great joy a son arrived on April 25th 1969, weighing in at over ten pounds.

*He's got the tiny little baby in his hands* ... That had been the key to unlocking John's heart at Harringay. Now it was as if God, the Father of life, had put the whole world of love and satisfaction into their hands, with this bouncing baby boy. They called him David, and prayed he would grow up to be a man after God's heart.

There was, however, one other hunger in John's life. On the human level he was doing well enough, as a senior executive of a multi-million pound company. His professional skill in property matters was of use as a consultant to Christian organizations, but it was at a personal level, where it counted, that he felt a failure. He wanted so desperately for people outside the churches to know what he knew, but he had no way to reach them.

Olga could communicate through helping to lead the 'Rendezvous' at Mitchley Hill Chapel, designed to reach women with no church attachment. John almost envied her—there was nothing like it for him to do...no way to reach the crowds in the shopping centres, and the neighbours in the houses around him, with the satisfaction he had found. There seemed to be unbridgeable gulfs. His private life was taken up by church activities and he had no interests to link him with his neighbours. The answer he found was Evangelism Explosion, a course of on-the-job training in personal witness.

David was turning out to be just the son John had dreamed of. A real boy, with the mischief and the disinclination for soap and water of the average youngster, but also a born leader, captaining and motivating the under 11 football team at school, and yet with a kind heart for those 'left out'. He forged bonds with his older sisters and their car-mad boyfriends and brought sunshine into all their lives.

So the conversation with new neighbours in Howard Road, Coulsdon one evening in early May, 1981, came as no surprise. The children were missing their old friends, the neighbours told John, but they were really pleased to have met David.

'Oh yes, he's my friend,' said a boy in the corner. John walked home thoughtfully, wishing he could make friends as easily.

He thought back to the happy party at their house just a week before—David's twelfth birthday coinciding with Jane's engagement to Keith, a young civil engineer and a Christian. Jane, nearly 22, was progressing at teacher training college and Sally, at 19, was living at home and starting a management course at Harrods. Trevor was in the picture there—also a keen Christian. How blessed they were in their children.

Next morning, just as David was settling down to his Saturday homework, his new friend came round to ask if he could go cycling. The younger boy had only just passed his proficiency test. Ever eager to put off homework, David jumped up: 'Oh, can I, Dad? We can go in the Drive.' The Drive was a quiet road nearby.

John sighed. The trouble he had on these Saturday mornings, getting the homework done. But he couldn't resist the appeal in the laughing eyes.

'Well—if you promise to get your homework done when you come back... and not stay out longer than an hour.'

David was halfway out of the door already. 'O.K....love you...' And he was gone.

Some minutes later the other boy's mother stood on the doorstep. She looked anxious.

'My son has just phoned to say they've had an accident. My husband's gone round to see to it.'

Her husband was a police officer concerned with traffic control.

John and Olga hurried down their front steps, and made for the car just as their neighbour came round the corner. He drove past the house and parked a little way up the road.

John went over. 'Is David O.K.?' he asked, not grasping the meaning.

The officer paused and took a deep breath: 'John—he's dead.'

Through the darkness that descended, Olga, John, Sally and Jane were conscious of the caring presence of their friends, bringing words of comfort and cups of hot tea. John, who had once faced death himself and had been scared enough to pray, looked out now into a world grown dark...stretched out his hands for a familiar grasp, and clutched empty air...listened for a quick footstep and a cheery young voice and heard only the silence.

It became a recurring nightmare, to his imagination... the quiet, twisting road...the parked cars...the sports car coming up the hill...the younger, less experienced cyclist in front braking suddenly...pedal clipping pedal...David thrown head on at the oncoming car.

Comfort came from an unexpected source. Edward Smith, formerly of the Hildenborough business committee, the speaker next day at Mitchley Hill Chapel, changed his sermon when he heard the news and told the congregation:

'I knew David—lovely boy. I remember the day at Bude CSSM when Oliver Styles the missionary told me that he had received a letter in the beach post box from David Lewis, who said he had given his heart to Jesus.'

A few days later, John felt strong enough to return to the scene of the accident. The sun was shining through the arch of trees overhead, the birds were singing their praises, and there was peace. John recalls his feelings:

'I stood by the police notice and I gazed up at the cathedral roof of trees over the road and the words came into my head, "Surely the Lord is in this place; and I knew it not...this is the gate of heaven" [Gen 28:16, 17]. I remembered where I had read them—in the *Daily Light* for May 2nd, the day David died. I had looked it up that very morning, but the words meant nothing to me.

'The thought came to me quite suddenly, "This is where Jesus put his hand down and scooped David up into heaven." It was inexpressibly comforting.'

Standing there he gave David back to God. Later that day he looked up the special passage for May 2nd in *Living Light*: 'God lives here. I've stumbled into his home. This is the awesome entrance to heaven.'

They became to him David's words, uttered at the moment he was snatched from death to a richer life.

Why do such tragedies happen? John is quite clear that while Christians are not exempt from the sufferings of mankind, they suffer for a purpose and receive power to turn sorrow to good account, on their own and others' behalf. He quotes: 'We do not want you to be ignorant about those who fall asleep, or to grieve like the rest of men who have no hope...' (1 Thess 4:13, NIV), and 'In all things God works for the good of those who love him, who have been called according to his purpose' (Rom 8:28, NIV).

David's loss, so shattering, has brought forth fruit in his family, unlocking their ability to meet other people's deepest questions, knowing that faith can penetrate the mystery, when understanding fails. John and Olga, Sally, Jane and their husbands have seen people come to a new experience of Christ's love through this seeming tragedy.

Meg, John's sister, who has also known her share of troubles in the years since Harringay, puts it like this: 'Everything was going well for them—nice house, good job, wonderful children. People would think, even if they didn't say it, "It's easy for you to be a Christian." People didn't listen to them as they do now. To experience a tragedy such as this and still believe in God's love, now that *is* a testimony.'

Recently the family felt the holding power of that love once again, when Jane became desperately ill. In this testing time, while John and Olga were counselling at the Luis Palau crusade in Croydon they were given just the tonic they needed—they saw three of David's greatest friends, and his teacher, walk forward to commit their lives to Christ.

And John, who is now involved in the leadership of the Evangelism Explosion training programme at Purley Baptist Church, says:

'When I look back to Harringay I know I was totally introverted with no real care for others. My focus was myself. Now I look outwards to other people and see them as those whom God loves and wants to forgive and make whole through his Son. God has my son, but he gave me his—and that makes all the difference.'

*Editorial Note:* Over 600 churches in twenty-two denominations are using the Evangelism Explosion training programme. Many formerly in decline are now growing. Address: 228 Shirley Road, Southampton, Hants SO1 3HR.

*'Commitment is the ability to stick patiently by your promise even when things are not working out as you had hoped'*

(Billy Graham).*

# 7

## How to Live Happily Ever After

Christina James was packing for a skiing holiday with her friend Anrôs. She was really looking forward to the break as life was rather a slog, though she loved her job teaching arts and crafts to pupils at St Paul's Girls' Prep School in Hammersmith.

She thought back to some years before when she had been a quiet, introverted teenager. Life had changed quite dramatically for Christina the night she followed her sister Penny's example at the Harringay crusade and had given her life to Christ. As a result their parents were now Christians too.

Would these old ski trousers of Father's do on the slopes? Oh well, they would have to, she thought. A newly qualified teacher's salary did not allow for splashing out on ski clothes, and it went against her thrifty nature to do so just for a holiday. She flung some old woollies into her hold-all then added paints and pastels in case she twisted an ankle while skiing! Her experience had in fact been confined to the golf course under snow.

*Copyright © Billy Graham Evangelistic Association.

At Victoria she met the others in the party—and for the first time clapped eyes on Anthony Bush, the young Somerset farmer Anrôs had mentioned: 'I think you'll like him,' her friend had said with a twinkle in her eye.

M-m-m, was Christina's first thought! Her second thought was—He's with someone else. Too bad. He seemed to be carrying another girl's luggage. She reminded herself that she had given up men for the time being, and was dedicated to her career and possible missionary work abroad.

'Matthew 6:33,' she murmured. This verse always came to her aid, convincing her that God would supply her deepest needs if she put his work first.

And yet she couldn't stop herself wondering if she'd ever meet anyone who was right for her. During her years of enjoyable, exciting, satisfying art training, no one quite qualified—and there had been no one in beach missions, youth clubs or church. Christian men were all either too superficial, too serious, too sold out on missionary work, or not sold out enough, rather humourless and stuffy, or already happily married. She dragged her mind back from this line of thought and struggled into a seat.

Anthony Bush's first thought had been: Wonder who that is? She looks nice. His second thought was: Too bad...she's with someone. That someone was carrying her luggage.

Anthony was on this holiday to look for a wife. It was tough keeping a farm on its feet, and he and his brother agreed that two comforting wives were badly needed in the freezing, empty farmhouse. 'It's better to marry than to freeze,' they laughed.

There had been plenty of applicants, of course, but a farmer's wife had to have more than a pretty face. She had to be resilient, resourceful, and know how to manage. And, even more important, Anthony wanted someone whose faith was real, and so would be true to him, as long as they both should live. He deposited the luggage he had been carrying, struggled into a seat—and found himself sitting next to Christina, who was, it turned out, un-escorted.

He had brought no food for the journey and was hungry, so Christina gave him some of her no-nonsense doorstep sandwiches. He liked that, and her air of reserve. Her shabby clothes, quite out of keeping with the après-ski atmosphere of the hotel, amused and interested him. When she duly twisted her ankle on the third day, he helped her back to the hotel and showed interest in her painting.

They went for evening walks, went dancing (Christina's ankle mended remarkably quickly!) and talked endlessly about themselves, their hopes and aspirations, aware all the time of the presence of the Creator and his master-plan in the surrounding snow and mountains.

Christina was blissfully happy, but remembered the story books. She knew that skiing holidays could be dangerously romantic. All the same, when walking home one evening Anthony had said in a throwaway manner, 'I shouldn't be surprised if I married you someday! Her heart lurched. But her head quickly took over and she replied: 'I'll let you off the hook if you change your mind when we get home.' She could have kicked herself for being such an idiot, and showing so little enthusiasm for someone who seemed so right for her.

On their last night Anthony said, 'Let's give ourselves a year' and she agreed. Christina knew a year would feel like eternity being both young and in love. But she also knew the story books didn't mention the quarrels and the heartbreak when people split up because they had rushed into a marriage without testing the attraction on which it was based.

Anthony went back to his freezing Somerset farmhouse, high on hills overlooking the Bristol Channel. It seemed bleaker than ever. Christina went back to art teaching and her church and youth work, trying to put him out of her mind, not daring to expect too much from a holiday romance.

They wrote to each other. They saw each other about once a fortnight, when he could spare time from the 250-acre farm. She became surer as time passed. He said little about the future—but they loved being together, and she fell in love with the old moated farmhouse, and with the countryside and culture of Somerset and Bristol.

Christina was finding the question of their future a test of faith and patience, but she kept her head, deciding to get out of London for the summer, to gather strength for her new challenging job in a rough Islington school in the autumn. Of Anthony there was no sign—he was busy with the harvest. Off to France she went to paint, unable to bear the waiting while he made up his mind.

When she got back there was an American at her door, sent by her sister Penelope, happily married to Tony Tyndale, with IVCF in Toronto.

To Christina this was a terrific diversion. She went round London with this very nice American for a few days and when Anthony got around to ringing to find out if she had come back, her flatmates kept him guessing: 'Sorry, she's taking this American out tonight'; 'Sorry, they're going to the theatre'.

Fortunately, the Dairy Show was on in London...and fortunately it was taking place next door to Christina's flat.

Christina had just stocked up the fridge with food and had changed for the evening when Anthony arrived, ostensibly for the Dairy Show, but in reality to find out what was going on. She was delighted to see him and he thought how sensible, comforting and pretty she was. And it was a few months later, outside Bristol railway station, that he put the momentous question: 'Christina, shall we get married?'

They then hurried to the farm to celebrate with brother John and his new fiancée, Pamela.

Anthony and Christina were married in February 1962, instantly forgetting loneliness, gloriously certain that this was God's plan for them—and trusting to live happily ever after!

The storm rolled in across the hills overlooking the Bristol Channel. John, their herdsman, had forecast a specially heavy storm. Christina had seen it coming too, but thought little about it, and went on preparing lunch for Mark and Andrew, the two farm students. There was no one else to prepare for that hot June morning in 1983. The family were scattered. Anthony was in Bristol, where he had been spending most of the hours, most days of the week, running the South-West regional office of Mission England, as its director. Lizzie was at Durham University, Annie had left for summer work in Ecuador with HCJB, Caspar was playing in a cricket match and Larry was at his school sports field, and would later need to be picked up.

Christina handed one of the students a copy of *Decision* magazine to read, as she went out to the farm office. Suddenly there was a terrific white flash around the telephone and the sound of a crash. Then silence. They guessed that lightning had struck nearby and Christina rushed back to the boys and begged them not to go out, for fear of being struck.

One of the students went to the front of the house, and then smelt burning and heard crackling up the stairs. Christina heard a shout: 'The roof's on fire!'

Christina grabbed the mercifully undamaged telephone to call the fire brigade, and then she phoned Anthony, while the boys did what they could with extinguishers to keep things under control, shutting doors, moving furniture and valuable treasures like photos and pictures.

Four fire engines dealt with the blaze, and while the men struggled to save the 400-year-old, three-storey farmhouse, Anthony and Christina sat on a stone wall companionably, drawn together by the drama.

God seemed very close, and gave peace. Christina found she had the copy of *Decision* in her hand, and pointed to the cover. It had a picture of a man running from lightning, and bore the legend: 'Is Judgement Coming?' Christina says now: 'It was almost funny, and we laughed, which must have appeared strange to an outsider. But marriage is about sharing—both jokes and sadness—and since no danger to life and limb was involved, laughter seemed quite good medicine for such an experience. We did feel sad, of course, about the loss of our children's personal possessions.'

Assessing it afterwards the fire chief pointed to massive oak beams built into the roof in medieval times. They were broken inwards, snapped like twigs.' He thought that the fire had been caused by 'a thunderbolt'. A fireproof carpet in the attic, and doors on the landing between the three floors had sealed the fire in, preventing it from advancing far downstairs in the ten minutes before they arrived. Only the roof was destroyed, and the ceiling and beams of the floor beneath.

Anthony and Christina looked at each other. How nearly they had taken out those doors, and blocked off that back staircase.

When in fact they looked at their insurance they found it specifically mentioned damage by 'lightning and thunderbolt', so they were covered. In fact, it was a terrific blessing in disguise: the part of the roof that was destroyed had dry rot and woodworm, and they had not been able to meet the cost of repair or make attic bedrooms comfortable.

It was a chaotic six months before the roof was snugly on again. After months with not enough bedrooms for everybody, Caspar camping in a caravan and water dripping through the roof and down the stairs, Christina took her Bible and went and lay down in the garden, and opened the pages at Psalm 23. She read the familiar words that laid their peace on her spirit:

'The Lord is my shepherd, I shall not want; he makes me lie down in green pastures, he leads me beside still waters' (RSV).

Lying down in their own green pastures, above the now calm waters of the Bristol Channel, and their own little moat, Christina drew strength as she meditated on this Psalm. And God spoke and lifted from her the burdens she had been carrying and reminded her of her priorities, and filled her with thankfulness for her family's safety, happiness and faith.

Christina started to think about their 'thunderbolt' in terms of some of the stories she had heard from others, who have difficulties and stresses in their lives. 'Thunderbolts don't ask permission—they strike at any time. What do we do then,' thought Christina, 'if we don't have our lives rooted firmly in Christ? Even happy marriages come under stress from time to time. It is hard to imagine families surviving these pressures without God keeping them together.'

She thought of all the times her family had laughed and cried together, and joined in some very practical praying round the big kitchen table over a new venture in the Pip 'n Jay Church in Bristol, a new foreign adventure of one of the family, plans for a barn party, plans for acquiring a double bass or a saxophone, a cow dying or having a difficult birth—all the complicated details of the hectic lives led by six busy people, friends and fellow-workers plus the extra children added to the family from time to time. With families as with farms you reaped the harvest you sowed.

The fire was a test—which they passed. But twelve years ago it was the marital failure they saw around them that prompted Christina and Anthony to start the Bristol Family Life Association.

Christina proposed the idea to Anthony after one of their evening walks to check on the dairy herd. 'Couldn't we form a group to educate people about the importance of marriage in society?' asked Christina.

'We could talk to schools, youth groups, men's and women's clubs,' she continued, 'and we could be a pressure group to protect the family.'

Anthony thought about the suggestion, and acted. The Bristol Family Life Association was founded in 1971 with a team of interested and influential people in the Avon and Somerset areas.

Ten years of this and Christina was convinced that education was not enough—people needed help in picking up the pieces—often reparable—before a crisis turned into divorce. There were very few Christian groups specializing in this area and they felt some non-Christian marriage guidance counselling appeared negative—often helping people along the road to divorce.

So, with friends in the Bristol Family Life Association, Christina and Anthony started Marriage Repair, a Christian counselling service, in 1981, eventually handing over the full responsibility to David and Christine Mitchell.

Their commitment to helping others with broken marriages comes from believing Jesus' teachings about the permanence of marriage. Anthony always tells people:

'Jesus' hard line against marriage after divorce, taken in the context of his day, when divorce was widespread, and marriage was largely arranged, and the wife a teenager, seems lacking in compassion. But his intention was to deter divorce and remarriage and encourage marriage, even if that meant hard work and a life of self-denial. So we see his true compassion was to prevent the divorcee's loneliness, and the suffering of the fatherless child, by preventing divorce.'

As a lay member of the General Synod, Anthony feels that the clergy could help marriages more than they do by refusing to marry divorcees in church. He supported a letter that went to every member of the Synod to ask them to keep the door open for a possible reconciliation, even after divorce.

He says: 'We know that Bristol Register Office remarry between six and twelve couples each year to each other, which casts doubt on the idea of irretrievable breakdown of marriage. In many cases if the door is left open and if there is a cooling off period, time for reconsideration and a time of separation, the couple may be able to work out how they can come together again, particularly if there are skilled counsellors available.'

Marriage Repair is advertised by posters in clinics, doctors' waiting-rooms, libraries, and often on radio or television programmes. A master phone with the number Bristol 424111 is linked with eight other phones, and telephone counsellors do a rota through the week. If more help is needed, visiting counsellors are called in to arrange a meeting to talk things over. After the number went in the phone book callers doubled.

Christina notes that not many Christians call, though, which is a pity. Christian marriages go wrong because they don't think they should have a problem and are too embarrassed to talk things over in the early stages.

Counsellors are chosen for maturity and marital background, and have undergone special training for the work. They meet regularly to pray about their work and problems. Trained advice comes from a solicitor, doctors, psychiatrist and several social workers.

Visiting counsellors have to be happily married, and most of them work with their own spouses in trying to help an inquiring couple. They have been chosen for their willingness to be unshockable in the counselling situation, for their commitment to repair even the most difficult marriage relationship. They are practitioners in prayer and are not afraid to talk to inquirers about the Christian faith, but only when it is appropriate.

What is a successful marriage? Marriage Repair states that it is where both partners are committed to each other, and to improving their marriage till death parts them. It should include a warm, emotional, spiritual and physical relationship, with plenty of communication and understanding. If there is disagreement, it should be in love. That kind of marriage is proof against fire, even though thunderbolts might strike.

Marriage Repair is proving its worth. Undoubtedly there are a good number of Bristol families now together and improving, since help from the service. Three-quarters of these are having long-term counselling.

The service often gets calls from people they have counselled. One such lady phoned them saying, 'I wanted to tell you that things are going very much better since we last met and talked. My husband seems to have become much more considerate since I finally dealt with my own problems, and the children are more settled and secure.

'God has helped me to forget the wrong in the past—and even my husband seems to be conscious of help that has been supernatural. It could only have been Christ's Holy Spirit which changed us. Please go on praying for us.'

*'Being a Christian is more than an instantaneous conversion—it is a daily process'* (Billy Graham).*

# 8

# *The Amazon Year*

'The voice of this hour...Billy Graham'. Radio Luxembourg cut through the babble of language coming from the speaker and young Trevor paused in his search along the wavebands. Billy Graham? His RE teacher had mentioned that name the other day: 'Billy Graham...a sort of John Wesley.' Tuning out the static, he settled to hear what this man had to say, pleased that his second-hand purchase, his pride and joy, was already proving an asset. He was the only boy in the class to own a radio, and this was the first chance he had to listen in.

The firm, confident voice of the man called Graham came loud and clear from the Hour of Decision into Trevor Allin's small bedroom. The boy listened, making no sense of it—until some familiar words came into focus:

'As many as received him to them gave he power to become the sons of God, even to them that believe on his name.'

*From Tony Castle (ed.), *The Hodder Book of Christian Quotations*, Hodder & Stoughton 1982.

He knew that by heart. He'd learned it for Christmas assembly.

Billy Graham was describing what it meant to be a son of God, a Christian. Nothing to do, apparently, with being born in a Christian country: 'If you were born in a garage would it make you a car?'

At the end of the talk there was a booklet on offer. Trevor sent for it.

Two weeks later, again alone in the room he shared with his twin brother, he studied the booklet on the Christian life according to Billy Graham. It talked about new life, self-surrender. A person could follow Christ emotionally or even intellectually, without becoming a born-again believer—that involved recognizing his need, understanding the meaning of the cross, counting the cost, and then taking a step of commitment to Jesus Christ.

The ideas dropped into his mind like stones in a pool, the ripples spreading. This Jesus, to whom he had never given a thought in his life, was real. He had died. He had come alive again and was calling *him*—Trevor Allin, a 15-year-old nobody, living on a council estate in Bromley, Kent. He was in the presence of a mystery. The room was very still.

'You can now pray and become a Christian,' said the booklet. Was it true? Yes, he believed it. Believing was the key to this mystery. Trevor fell to his knees, and in halting words handed over his life as best as he knew how. It was December 3rd 1960. He knew he had switched on to God but certainly could not forsee how many other lives were to be altered as a result.

Church had never appealed to Trevor, but the next day was Sunday and he had to find an explanation for this peace and joy that had taken possession of his life. Even in the tense atmosphere of home he found himself smiling.

He found a church where everything was made clear. The fellowship at Downham Baptist Church welcomed Trevor, and Brian, his inseparable twin. It was like finding a second family, with ties of spirit not blood, and with whom one had no quarrels. Trevor dug out his Bible and found there hope and promise. He went on listening to and learning from Christian radio programmes. His new security only served to underline the unhappiness at home where his parents' marriage was wearing thin. There was no easy escape from incompatibility in those days. Trevor was too young to understand the causes. He knew only the pain.

At Malory Comprehensive School Trevor's headmaster was a veteran of the Spanish Civil War. That campaign, a rallying ground for idealists, cost the lives of many and left others disillusioned. Mr McCarthy, surveying his pupils, knew that they were capable of good and bad, and created a climate of discipline to bring out the good. From his study, via microphone and speakers, he could address every classroom at once keeping 1,000 pupils pinned to their seats at assembly, listening. When it was pointed out to him that Trevor Allin, a reasonably able but shy lad in the fourth year was now telling everyone, including his teachers, that they should believe in Jesus Christ, the head thought about it carefully, and then surprised Trevor by inviting him to lead three assemblies on Monday mornings—the first time in living memory it had been done by a pupil.

Trevor took along Brian and two or three others of his class who had come under his influence. Long after he recalled what he felt:

'We read from Peter's sermon on the day of Pentecost—shortened because it was too long for a ten-minute assembly. Someone said a prayer and I spoke for a few minutes to all 1,000 children. It was quite an awe-inspiring experience for me to sit in front of a microphone in the headmaster's study and speak to the whole school.'

Within a few months the head made Trevor a prefect—evidence from an objective source that God had taken charge and was making something of him.

Six months after the life-changing radio broadcast Billy Graham arrived in person to hold a crusade in Manchester. The YPF went as a group to the relay services in Bromley Baptist Church and first Brian and then Vera, their 14-year-old sister, made a personal commitment to Jesus Christ.

Until then Brian had shadowed Trevor, but June 7th 1961 was a date that had a profound effect on his life. Brian says today:

'It was the first time I realized that Christ had come to save me, and that I was a sinner who needed saving. That was a revolutionary thought. Billy spoke so clearly and sharply, as if he were speaking only to me.'

Trevor started getting up at 6.30 a.m. each day to read the Bible and talk to God—arming against those moments of doubt when he wondered if his new-found faith was just some gigantic idea thought up by Billy Graham. But he always returned to words he knew by heart: 'He that hath the Son hath life; and he that hath not the Son of God hath not life' (1 Jn 5:12, AV). God said it so it must be true.

It was around this period their mother left them. Trevor did not know where she was. His older sister Jean had already left home in bitterness, leaving no forwarding address. The three teenagers clung to God, listening for his voice in prayer times together before they went about their daily occupation. It gave them the support they needed.

By the time Trevor was 17, he had a job in the Inland Revenue, with security for life. But it was about this time that an electrifying young man, George Verwer, made good use of a ten-minute spot at a Youth For Christ meeting to talk about Operation Mobilization. Trevor was riveted. Quietly, he decided on his next move.

Colleagues at work, when he announced he was leaving to go to France with Operation Mobilization, tried to discourage him. His father and sister said he was being 'extreme'.

The *Bromley Advertiser* got hold of the story and printed it prominently, with a picture of a well-brushed young man in a neat, dark suit. The text ran:

'A 17-year-old Bromley boy is to give up his job in the Civil Service so that he can give all his time this summer to a crusade to take the gospel to the peoples of the Continent.

'He is Trevor Allin of Ivorydown, a member of Bromley Youth for Christ and the Baptist Church.

'The aim of the Crusade, called Operation Mobilisation, is to distribute 200 tons of literature, comprising 250 million pages.

'It is planned to work in five countries... but Trevor will probably go to France as he learned the language at school. All members will be taught fifty phrases in the language of the country they visit.

'Trevor says: "My role will be that of foot soldier. I think of climbing stairs and ringing doorbells, standing in markets and on street corners for eight or nine hours a day, and I know it will not be easy. But then I think of the 141 million souls living in the five countries and I know that the majority of them have never once heard a clear presentation of the way of salvation.

'"We hope to co-operate as much as possible with local churches, and when we leave we hope that the Christians there will continue our work so there will not be just a void."'

Trevor's mother, who had not seen her son for two years, cut out the interview and kept it among her papers.

Three months in France extended to a year. Trevor returned home adult and confident, having learned to trust God to meet basic day-to-day needs. He had preached in French to Swiss students on the steps of Lausanne University, discussed his faith with students in Marseilles and Dijon, and helped individuals take the first steps into a new Christian life. He now had a clear aim— to improve on his nine O-levels and head for university to read modern languages, as Francis Schaeffer of L'Abri and Jonathan McRostie of Operation Mobilization had encouraged him to do. If he could do this, he would be the first member of the Allin family to go to university and, more important than this, be better equipped to spread the gospel.

Trevor had learned with Operation Mobilization that the Christian life is one of love and reconciliation, so decided to try to repair the rift with his mother and elder sister. Jean had gone abroad, but he began to visit his mother regularly. It was difficult for Trevor to understand all that had gone on in the past, but with new eyes he came to see that war years, and the separation from her husband for three years at a stretch, and the problems of rearing four children had not made life plain sailing.

One year later, having achieved the necessary A-levels by correspondence, Trevor arrived at Leeds University to study French, Spanish, phonetics, and philosophy and history of religion. The idea of going to South America was beginning to crystallize—he had heard from Wycliffe Bible Translators that there were small tribes tucked away in the jungles, speaking inaccessible languages, with no written form, and therefore with no possibility of having the Bible. Trevor knew how basic the Bible was to belief—he had read it through seven times.

In 1967 Billy Graham was back in England, at Earls Court, and Mrs Allin went to the crusade with a coachload from Christ Church, Bromley.

That meeting, on July 1st, clinched the changes that had been taking place in her life over several months. Returning home four weeks later Trevor found a different mother, and a new basis to their relationship:

'I learned something new then,' he says today. 'I learned that one of the first things you do when you become a Christian is to say "sorry" to God for the sins you have committed. For the first time in my life I heard my mother say "I'm sorry".'

Spain beckoned Trevor, who now needed to acquire fluency in Spanish for his degree course. He found it in Malaga working as a language assistant in a secondary school, then at the British Consulate, sorting out visitors' problems.

He was helped towards his first-class honours degree by an essay on Martin Luther's theme of justification by faith, which he was able to translate into personal experience:

'I saw so clearly that it was not something invented by Martin Luther, nor by Billy Graham...it is a doctrine perceived by true Christians down the ages, but which each person has to find for himself or herself. It is possible to miss it, even while calling yourself a Christian.'

His second year in Malaga, after his finals, working in a school and with the British Consulate, provided him with a plateau from which to view the future. Trevor remembered the Alps seen from Huemoz, and the words of Dr Francis Schaeffer:

'Go for the highest of which you're capable. God wants us to use our intellectual abilities for his glory. Get a degree and then go and serve the Lord.'

He was just about to climb a new peak—research into linguistics for a PhD at St Andrews University. At this point he became aware of the beautiful, dark-haired,

Maria Victoria.

She was a secretary, daughter of a respected Malaga businessman, and he was her English teacher.

Just at that time some missionaries asked Trevor to translate into Spanish a Bible correspondence course. Trevor asked Maria Victoria if she would check his work, and so, after the English class, they regularly got out the correspondence course and a Spanish Bible. The friendship slowly deepened.

Maria Victoria became increasingly more involved in the life of the local fellowship of Christians, where she appeared to be perfectly at home. He went ahead prayerfully with the friendship.

The course at St Andrews University Centre for Latin American Linguistic Studies took three years, one of which had to be spent out in the field.

Trevor prefaced it with a three months' course at the Wycliffe Summer Institute of Linguistics. He was then accepted by Wycliffe to do his research year, working with them as a short-term assistant in Peru. His task would be to produce a linguistic analysis and dictionary of a language spoken by a small tribal group—too small for Wycliffe's over-stretched full-time workers to tackle, but still needed.

A year later he arrived at Brillo Nuevo, a small Indian village on the banks of the Yaguasyacu river, a tributary of the mighty Amazon. He was to work initially with Wes and Eva Thiesen, two Wycliffe translators, who were just finishing twenty years' work on the Bora New Testament. The new recruit was impressed by the rich culture and friendliness of the Bora tribe, and by the dedication of the two missionaries.

The Indian houses, with their walls of tree bark, were on stilts because of frequent flooding. There was a church on stilts with a roof of poles and palm leaves which kept off the downpour admirably. The Indians crowded in to hear preaching and singing by Boras who had been led to the Lord by Wes and Eva. For the two missionaries preached with their lives: love was a language all could read.

Later Trevor left the Thiesens to move up-river to the Ocaina village of Puerto Izango. 'Izango means mosquito' he was told—and it was true! Among the Ocaina lived eight people, who spoke a language, Resigaro, thought to be a dialect of Bora. One of them was Pablo, a young man of about 20 who spoke a little Spanish, learned in a bilingual school established by Wycliffe in collaboration with the Peruvian government. He told Trevor that there were more people speaking their language, Resigaro, over the border in Colombia.

The village consisted of a few houses and the school, which had a roof, but no walls. Trevor moved into a house on stilts with an Indian family. It had one main room, in which he was allotted a piece of floor space to spread his sleeping bag and hang up a mosquito net. He had forgotten to pack a mirror, so he grew a beard. After a few weeks he went barefoot like the Indians.

They cooked food for him—boiled turtle, roast monkey, pineapples, and he paid them, doubling their income in that very marginal economy. Trevor longed, though, to be able to communicate with these friendly Indians.

One evening, he brought out the second-hand tape-recorder bought from a missionary at Wycliffe's office in Lima, and set it down. The Indian family gathered around, their dark eyes fastened on him curiously, to see what wonder he would work. He tried to remember what he had to do next.

Going through the tropical vocabulary designed for such moments he obtained the words for body parts—toe, hand, foot, head, finger. Then the elements—water, air, fire. Then food, palm tree. The Indians warmed to it, and when he played it back to them they laughed shyly.

'Do you want a story?' said Pablo, and his sister Adelina launched into story telling. She told twenty stories, in a beautiful clear voice. She sang songs to him, traditional songs, going back hundreds of years.

Months later, when he knew some Resigaro, Pablo and he were listening to those tapes, and Pablo said:

'I don't understand that word. We don't use some of those words any more.' Trevor, with a thrill of discovery, realized he was experiencing the strength of oral tradition. The language of ordinary life had simplified, but the old words still remained in a tribal memory bank, to be handed down, usually from mother to daughter.

If Adelina got a word wrong in telling her stories, there was her mother, interrupting and correcting, according to the traditional version. It was a strong argument for the truth of the Bible, with its stories of Genesis and the Flood, and its reports of all that Jesus did and said, carried in people's memories word for word before anything was written down.

Pablo and Trevor worked at transcribing the stories. Pablo, he found, was an intelligent informant. Trevor had to devise an orthography for writing down Resigaro, which he did, basing it on a modified form of the International Phonetic Alphabet. Trevor paid for most of Pablo's food and gave him the equivalent of 5p an hour— half his disposable income. He explained carefully to the Indian that in spite of having a watch, camera and tape recorder he had no more cash than that.

They went together to Wycliffe base camp at Yarina-cocha where problems could be sorted out with senior translators. There they found other short-term assistants helping in a variety of ways as Trevor was doing. One young butcher had come from America to give a year of service with food supplies for the 250 members and children serving in Peru. Wycliffe always needed people with everyday skills as well as translators.

At first he and Pablo spoke to each other in Spanish, but towards the end they were speaking in Resigaro.

The objective was to compile a 2,000 word dictionary, but in off-duty hours he and Pablo translated the first four chapters of Mark's Gospel. It was all that could be done in a year, and the Gospel could not be published, without stringent tests on grammar and phonetics.

Their translation of Mark 1:1 ('This is the beginning of the gospel of Jesus Christ, God's Son') read like this: 'Gihi neeihpe gikelloh kaásho tsopókó Jesucristo iihñé Vakéllohtoonagí ihyaání.' (This it began long ago the faithful message of Jesus Christ our Creator's Son.)

To the last, Trevor was discovering ten or twelve new words a day. But his year was up. He and Pablo parted with sorrow—they had been partners in this Wycliffe enterprise. He had reduced the basics of a language to writing. If he could, he would have stayed on then.

The thesis for Trevor's doctorate took three years, instead of one, and it ran to over 500 pages. In 1972 he married Maria Victoria, and brought her to St Andrews and then to Perth. He taught Spanish and French while he finished 'A Grammar of Resigaro'.

It was eventually completed, and was printed at Wycliffe's UK headquarters at High Wycombe. Two hundred copies went to Peruvian universities and libraries. One hundred copies of the 150-page vocabulary went to the Peruvian government and, combined with a Spanish introduction and a new cover, became an official Wycliffe publication.

St Andrews University awarded Trevor Allin his PhD. He had earned it. Pablo caught the thirst for knowledge, and Trevor gladly paid for his education through years of primary and then secondary school, so that he could get to the standard required of a village primary school teacher, which he reached in 1983.

But life was not without problems. Trevor and Maria Victoria found themselves drifting apart. Communication had broken down. She hated the English weather and felt that people were unfriendly. Churchgoing, which had played such a part in their courtship and early marriage, dropped to second place, now they had a baby in the house. Trevor was busy at school, with a heavy work commitment.

They needed help. One Sunday morning at their church in Sible Hedingham, their minister, George Balfour, asked couples to come forward to rededicate their marriages. Maria Victoria taking the initiative, grabbed Trevor's hand and they went to the front.

'We asked the Lord to love us and forgive us and help us really be united,' says Trevor. 'It made all the difference to us and our little Angela who came to the Lord. We now make time each day for family worship, and it draws us together. We often hold hands as we pray, and we share everything with the Lord, trusting him for the future.'

The power of God's forgiveness came home to him once again in 1982 when his mother died of cancer. It was a harrowing time for the whole family but Mrs Allin pillowed her head on Jesus' words in John 14:2, 3: 'I go to prepare a place for you.' Paul's great declaration of faith was especially precious in the last few days: 'There is therefore now no condemnation for those who are in Christ Jesus' (Rom 8:1, RSV). She passed away secure in that knowledge.

Today the family is scattered: Vera is on the OM ship *Doulos* with her husband Michael Peevor and their baby son; Brian is a partner in an international firm of accountants based in Johannesburg. He and his wife Wendy have two children. They all keep in touch—the bonds are strong. They pray for their elder sister Jean who is abroad somewhere.

Trevor plays a key role in his community. He is head of modern languages in his comprehensive school, chairman of the Town Twinning Association, and in May 1983 he ran for the Halstead Town Council as a ratepayer with the backing of his church and now serves as a councillor. He spends time each week helping people with personal problems.

'For choice, I would have gone back to Peru, ten years ago, since I rate agencies such as Wycliffe vital in reaching those who have never had a chance to hear the gospel, but circumstances dictated otherwise.' Though his work among the Resigaro-speaking natives was both important and exciting, he accepts that active Christians are needed in every sphere of society, and especially in schools, where young lives are shaped for the future. His input to his pupils includes helping them to see beyond the differing language and culture, not foreigners but brothers.

'I have proved, from Halstead to the rain forests of Peru, that people are the same under the skin, with the same needs, the same fears.

'By their own standards they do things that are wrong. They need forgiveness, reassurance and comfort, are frightened of dying and have difficult personal relationships, where forgiving helps, and Christ's love is the real answer to life's most acute problems. With him people can grow to their full potential.'

And but for the twist of a dial on a second-hand radio he might never have known.

*Editorial note:* Wycliffe Bible Translators has about 4,500 workers from twenty-three countries working in 750 languages. A New Testament takes up to fifteen years to complete and 200 have been published. Some 3,000 languages still need Bible translation, representing at least 200 million people. There are over 1,000 vacancies for translators, literacy and support workers. Address: Horsleys Green, High Wycombe, Bucks HP14 3XL.

Operation Mobilization has about 1,700 workers from thirty-five countries working in some twenty-five countries. The emphasis is on training and evangelism. As well as land teams, there are also two ships—*Logos*, which has 140 workers on board, and *Doulos*, with over 300. All are 'volunteers'. In addition, many young people join OM for a one or two-month summer campaign. Address: 142 Dantzic Street, Manchester M4 4DN.

*'We have not yet learned that a person is more powerful when he is at prayer than when he is in control of the most powerful military weapons we have ever developed'* (Billy Graham).*

# 9

# *Across the Borders*

The idea that Pastor John Edwards should visit Christians behind the Iron Curtain in person was born one November, and no one then foresaw how big the outcome would be.

The Full Gospel Church, Dennett Road, Croydon, already had links with an East German Pentecostal church, through a twinning scheme run by the European Missions department of the Assemblies of God. So far they had been able to send their twin church food and a washing-machine by arrangement with an export firm. Thinking about this, and about the approaching Christmas season, a idea took shape in his mind—and he tried it out on Doris, his wife.

'Why don't I try and visit our twin church? It would encourage the local Christians, wouldn't it?'

'Good idea,' said Doris. 'We could send something for the children.'

Their church was fired with enthusiasm for the project and discussed what they could send. But almost

* *Decision* magazine.

117

immediately a snag arose—it was going to be difficult to stay in East Germany, except in hotels. The authorities wanted Western currency.

Since the idea was to visit the Christians, that was a non-starter. They were praying this over when Joseph, a young man in the church, came up with an alternative suggestion:

'If East Germany is impossible, why not try Poland? Poland is 250 miles further on, but you will find many Christians in the Evangelistic Union and there are no such restrictions on visiting.' They would, however, have to pay £8 a day just to stay there.

Joseph had come from Poland to train at Bible college in Sussex. Despite pressure to return home he had been granted leave to stay by the Home Office and was now beaming back Polish broadcasts, via IBRA Radio in Sweden, and working among Slavs in England.

The Evangelistic Union, John knew, was made up of several evangelical denominations: Brethren, Churches of Christ, Baptist and Pentecostal. Over recent years the Pentecostal Church had proved itself the fastest-growing segment of the Union, and the people were hungry for teaching. This, then, was the answer.

The church collected children's clothes and woollens for Poland and the children in the Sunday school and club brought their sweets and these were packed into a house-shaped container for the twin church in East Germany. Ian James, a young man in the church, offered to go with the pastor to deliver the goods.

Visas were obtained, currency bought, and the Renault was checked over. The two men listened to advice:

They had to get transit visas for East Germany at the border. They would not be allowed to stay overnight, unless they slept at hotels. They ought not to leave the motorway, and would have to produce receipts, date-stamped for where they stayed.

There were problems keeping within these restrictions—Bruno, the pastor they were looking for, spoke no English, so they had first to find his brother Dieter, also a pastor, in another town 30 miles away, to act as interpreter.

But John reassured friends who expressed concern. 'It'll be all right,' he said. It was his usual statement of faith, born of years of experience in Christian service.

All the same he noted a prophecy, delivered by a lady in the church the Sunday before they set out: 'Men will try to turn you aside. You are to continue.'

The weather was fine, sunny and dry as they drove through West Germany towards the East German border. Filling the boot and the back seat of the Renault were five boxes, one black plastic bag, a 'house' filled with sweets, and their own personal bags.

Then, without warning, came trouble—a knocking in the engine. Pulling off the autobahn into the next garage they learned the worst. One of the cylinder piston rings had broken, and it would cost a lot to repair. Even worse, it would take time.

John asked if the repair could be done immediately but the mechanic shook his head. It was now Friday evening and the repair shop was closed until Monday morning.

This was bad news, but John was not a man to become apprehensive.

'I think we should go on,' he said to his companion. 'It'll be all right.' He happened to believe in miracles, having seen a few happen in his time.

Ian grinned. 'Yes,' he said, 'we've had the promise, haven't we?'

John had forgotten about the prophecy until that moment but, heartened by this, he started the motor and they clattered out of the garage, leaving the mechanic staring in amazement after them.

The lights marking the border between the West and East Germany had long since slipped away behind them. The car was by now making a dreadful noise, like a tractor, and drinking vast quantities of oil. They stopped frequently at garages along the autobahn to replenish the supply. Still they kept going on three cylinders, aided by some fervent praying.

Late that night they neared the turn-off for the town where the pastor lived. 'Not quite as planned, but here goes,' said John, and took the turning. They crawled through a maze of badly lit streets, lost and cutting a swathe of sound through the night.

When they got to what they judged to be the town centre, John stopped the car and Ian got out and showed the address they sought to one or two people. They denied all knowledge of it.

'Help us, Lord,' said John.

Almost immediately a post office van pulled up in front of them and the driver got out. Ian walked up to him, holding out the paper with the address.

The postman looked at it briefly, consulted his watch, and then beckoned. They clattered after the van, as it threaded out of the city centre and through the suburbs.

The van stopped outside a small bungalow. This was it. They thanked their guide and handed him some chocolate bars—'For your children', they explained.

A smile lit up his face. 'Danke schön', said the man, and drove off.

John and Ian approached the door and knocked. It was opened by a young woman. She stood uncertainly in the lighted hallway. She spoke no English, and it took her a few moments to grasp who they were. Then her face lit up with pleasure.

When the pastor arrived home a short time later, he was taken completely by surprise: 'How wonderful you are here. Praise the Lord.'

Before they could talk, though, they had to park the car out of sight in a garage behind the bungalow.

The Pastor Dieter was a great encouragement to their faith. He was full of rejoicing in what God was doing in his church, especially among the young people, in spite of limitations. Among the restrictions he lived with was that permission had to be obtained for a visiting speaker.

But there was no doubt about it. His church was growing, and attracting people who were hungry for food for their souls. The diet of materialism gave no nourishment. As he listened John felt he was receiving more from this man than he could possibly give in return.

Early the next morning, Dieter took them in his car to the next town to find his brother Bruno at the twin church. There John and Ian delivered the gifts from the Sunday school and added three of the boxes of woollens. Again there was a touching amazement and gratitude that they had come.

The Pentecostal church was impressive—a large pre-war building, with two halls, a large room underneath, and a flat on top. 'We could do with this in Croydon,' exclaimed John. His own church had no room to grow.

John and Ian learned that 100 people came to two services on Sunday. There were well-attended weeknight meetings also, for Bible study, prayer and for the youth. In addition, they had the charge of a small church up in a mountain village, with thirty adults and a large Sunday school, bigger than the one in town. They would receive the sweets from the Croydon Sunday school, the pastor and his wife decided.

There was a time of prayer that will remain for ever engraved in John's mind, but all too soon it was time to leave. He expressed his regrets.

'You have blessed us in that you cared enough about us

to come in person,' replied Bruno.

The car sounded no better, though, as, later that day, they resumed their journey to the Polish border. They slowly covered the miles, willing the rattling engine not to die on them.

After four hours they reached the German border, its checkpoint manned with soldiers.

'Where did you spend last night?' the guard asked, as he looked at the date-stamps on their transit visas.

They could not lie, but were resolute that they should not cause trouble to their hosts of the night before.

John pointed to the engine. 'Caput—trouble!' he said.

The guard was not impressed. 'Where did you sleep?', he persisted, using sign language to make them understand.

There was no way out. John mentioned the town.

'Ah, a hotel...the papers?' the guard continued.

'No, not a hotel,' answered John.

The guard was becoming increasingly impatient. The situation was growing tense. Obviously not satisfied by their answers, he took their passports and visas and walked away into the guard house.

'He's gone to get someone who speaks English,' said John.

And yet there was a sense of peace in his heart as he prayed for the outcome. A few minutes later, another guard emerged, carrying their passports. They braced themselves for the explanations.

The guard came up to the car and looked them over. Then he handed their documents to John—and laughed.

'Have a happy holiday,' he said, and waved them on.

On the Polish side of the border the checkpoint guards passed them through without even examining the boxes.

*Bang! Flash!* The piston blew out of the bottom of the engine, and the car clattered to a halt. One look around was enough—it was a pitch dark, cold, wet night and they were stranded in the middle of the Polish countryside, 200 miles from Warsaw.

Not very hopefully, Ian stood by the side of the Auto-bahn to thumb a lift. The road was quiet, but the very first car that approached slowed down. The four people inside sized up the situation and Ian disappeared with them into the night.

In less than an hour Ian was back, with a towing truck from the state-run breakdown service and a cheery driver who linked them to his vehicle and towed them to the next town. He put the car in a hotel car park for the night, explaining that it was unsafe to leave it on the streets:

'You come back…the wheel's gone.'

But they had to get to Warsaw. The breakdown driver had a solution for that too—he took them to the railway station, and bought their tickets for Warsaw. They paid him for his services, and loaded themselves and their remaining boxes and bags thankfully into the crowded train.

The train left at midnight for the eight-hour journey. They were wedged in a restaurant car, with standing room only. People looked at them curiously—two crumpled foreigners, in need of a shave, with large quantities of luggage.

Suddenly, a great, burly waiter beckoned them into the corridor. He pushed through the crowd and stopped before a compartment and flung open the door. It was jammed tight with bodies as far as John and Ian could see, but their friend dived in and ordered people to move up. Miracu-lously, two seats appeared. The boxes were stowed on racks or their laps and with smiles to all around they tried to relax. The waiter walked away, refusing a tip.

It was a night to remember, squeezed between the sleeping Polish travellers. The train was slow and stopped at what seemed like every station. The lady sitting next to John kept glancing at his baggage...she looked as if she wanted to buy something.

John's thoughts turned to Doris and the way in which she had stood beside him all these years. He knew that her prayers surrounded him now. And gradually, with the gentle rhythm of the train's wheels on the tracks, he lost himself in the unrolling vision of his life....

He was 9 years old and he was up in the balcony at Harringay with his mother. Down below Billy Graham was making an appeal and people were going forward. He started to fidget. 'For goodness' sake sit still!' his mother hissed.

He was, in fact, trying to get up off his seat and go forward with the other people who were crowding to the front. But he sat still. The moment for decision passed and he went out of that meeting a rather sad little boy. It never entered his head that this was the same message preached at chapel. Harringay, for him, was the place of opportunity.

Then one day he heard the Wembley Sunday school was going to Harringay, and with eagerness he awaited the day.

The meeting began with singing, jokes and laughter. Then came Billy, holding out a big Bible, even larger than the pastor's at chapel. He thumped it and waved his arms. Now the moment had arrived when he was going to give his life to Jesus. He didn't wait for anyone else—he just ran straight down the stairs and to the front, and committed his life for ever.

There was no real sense of 'before' and 'after'. But his ambition grew towards being a preacher, just like Billy Graham.

Years later he was to tell his mother about it: 'When

we had a preacher and I knew what the reading was I'd be working out in my mind his next points and what else he could have said.'

He passed through all the stages—children's meeting, youth meeting and then to the open-air meeting at Speaker's Corner, Hyde Park, on Sunday afternoons. At 14 or 15 it took guts to stand against the heckling and give a testimony.

Uncle Eddie had started a church in the suburbs of Brussels at the end of the war, and added a youth camp and old folks' home. John joined him, learned French and was there for nearly a year working with his uncle.

But by the time he was 21 he felt that he ought either to earn a living or to get some kind of further training for Christian service. So back in England he joined an Assemblies of God church in South Harrow. It was an important move for him—Pastor George Rutherford taught the gifts of the Spirit and the life of the Spirit.

There he gained what had been lacking in his experience—the power of the Holy Spirit and a deeper knowledge of the Bible. The pastor encouraged him to preach and lead meetings, and it was at South Harrow in 1966 that he had met Doris.

After they were married they tried to settle down to Uncle's work in Belgium, but support was lacking—people didn't think of Europe then as a mission field. They came home after a year.

But John felt the call to preach even more strongly. Encouraged by George Rutherford, he applied to the Home Missions department of the Assemblies of God to become a pioneer pastor. He was sent to a new church in Wrexham and then to Gainsborough, Lincolnshire where he rescued a dying church.

And so by stages he came to the Croydon Full Gospel Church, who were looking for just such a young and energetic pastor. There were forty people in the congregation on his first Sunday; now after ten years there were about 260 on Sunday mornings and they had outgrown the building.

The train was approaching Warsaw, and John was suddenly jolted back into the present. The other travellers also awoke, stretched their cramped limbs, gripped their luggage and prepared to struggle off the train. John and Ian gathered everything up and, disembarking, found a taxi.

And so, finally, John and Ian reached the house of Joseph's brother Peter and met with the warmest of welcomes from Christians, which the Full Gospel Church had prayed for so many times.

They then learned just how much God's hand had been on their journey across Eastern Europe. Throughout the country the garages were state run. Only a few were privately owned, and the town where their car was waiting boasted one of these—and it happened to be owned by a member of the Pentecostal church. It was a simple matter to arrange the repair with some telephoning.

The car was ready in three days. Meanwhile, Joseph's brother took time off work and introduced them to churches in the area, where they were able to speak. When they collected the car they had a further surprise. The young garage owner had been able to obtain a new Renault engine from Rumania, another Eastern bloc country, at a very favourable exchange rate. It cost them the equivalent of £150. (It would have cost more than three times that in West Germany.)

The evangelicals here too he found had a very positive attitude to their circumstances. They had learned, as one pastor put it, to live within their limitations, but they knew the power of prayer.

During the ten days in Poland they were able to visit seven churches, preaching through an interpreter. There were always eager young folk able to translate. 'Our young people like to learn English,' he was told. The chance might come to go to America, where so many of their relatives lived. Even as John and Ian waved goodbye to them and set off on the long trek homewards, John was planning, in faith, a second trip to Poland.

And in August, he did just that. But this time, by special invitation, he took Doris; they were there for two weeks.

The third visit was in the following October, with one of the church officers, John Weatherlay. It was the time that food shortage troubles were beginning. When they realized the desperate need they made arrangements for another trip in December, and took the church mini-bus piled high with a ton and a half of food and clothing. They left Poland on Thursday and got home on Saturday night. On Sunday morning the news came over the BBC that martial law had been declared, and that Poland was now ruled by a military government.

John immediately contacted the Polish Embassy to ask if they could visit with more food and clothing. Permission was granted, and in January they set off with three full mini-buses. The gifts were not just from John's own church. Other churches in the Croydon area heard of his trip and collected items. Boxes were put out at local schools for children's clothes. Baptists, Methodists and Anglicans collected at their Sunday services.

Eastern Europe was in the grip of snow and ice, and the temperature was minus 20 at the border.

John and his party arrived in Cracow about midnight, tired and uncertain as to what sort of a reception they would get. They found their way barred by the militia. An interpreter was found and John explained their mission.

'We have these goods to deliver to a friend, and we would like to stay with him,' he told them. 'Oh that's fine,' they said, and were very pleased when they handed them some bars of chocolate and tins of meat.

An officer then told them to follow him in their vans. He drove in front of them through the empty streets. At about one o'clock they arrived at Edward's house. They knocked but got no answer. The militia man knocked too, and called out to him in Polish. Then they saw Edward peeping out the window, looking frightened, and John called his name.

He saw them and answered the door. 'Chwala Bogu,' he exclaimed—'Praise the Lord!' Later he explained that he thought the soldiers had come for him because he had been trying to get the police that week to release a consignment of paper he had been sent from the West to print some literature.

John and his helpers went once more in October 1982 with another three van loads. This time there was a brush with the secret police when they tried to take pictures of a horse market.

There were delays at checkpoints after this. Guards ordered everything to be unpacked. After this they discovered a better way of getting out supplies: via a Polish transporter firm, based in London. Their next visit had a different purpose.

In April 1983 John held a seminar in a town near the Czech border. A friend from Cracow had hired three holiday homes and about sixty people came together for a week of meetings. Andrew Shearman of Talbot Street, Nottingham, and leader of International Outreach, joined him. John recalls: 'We didn't know what to expect, but it was a tremendous time. We had the seminars in the mornings and afternoons and in the evenings went out to local churches and took meetings. There was a Lutheran church up in the hills with about fifty people there, and some Pentecostal churches in the area with 100 or 200 people in the congregation. The majority of the people we spoke to had been Christians for less than a year. Many of the churches in Poland have doubled and doubled again in the last two years. It seems that all the troubles in the country have just made people more receptive. We spoke a lot about faith—believing the Lord and taking him at his word, and encouraging people to praise. It brings the power of God into all our lives.

'We have noticed a great change in attitude on the part of the authorities to the evangelicals in Poland over the past two years. They seem ready now to allow the hire of the biggest halls in towns and swimming pools for baptismal services.'

Looking back over his life since Harringay, John sums it up:

'The Lord brings to pass the things we hope for. I hoped for a gospel ministry. Now with a strong church behind me the Lord has opened such a ministry. The gospel crosses all borders. No barriers—political or ideological—can prevent the Spirit of God from moving throughout the world.'

*'To reach the greatest heights...a person must learn how to take advantage of a difficulty'* (Billy Graham).*

# 10

# *Action Man*

As Christopher Russell sees it, if ministers were to apply business management skills as well as faith to their work there would be less talk of retreat or decline and more growth through sharing of resources. He believes in putting the domino theory into reverse—making small churches stand up, with a little help from their friends. During the past twenty years as a minister he has been planting churches at a time when many small Baptist churches were closing.

His story begins in a relay service in Harlington Baptist Church, Middlesex, in May 1955, when, as a 13-year-old boy, he listened to Billy Graham speaking from the Kelvin Hall, Glasgow. The large church was unusually packed for the occasion.

Of the power that drew him down the aisle at the appeal, Christopher says: 'I wasn't listening to Billy Graham: I heard the voice of the Holy Spirit asking me to repent of my sins and surrender my life.'

The minister at Harlington, the Reverend Bob Browell,

* *Till Armageddon*, Hodder & Stoughton 1981.

131

was leaving and suggested to Christopher that he wait for his successor before being baptized. Meanwhile, the young people's team had an injection of Billy Graham converts who took services in small churches in the Heathrow flight-path area. Sometimes speakers would be forced to stop for ten seconds every two minutes, as the planes screamed overhead. Christopher, who was often in the pulpit, learned to conquer panic and began to master a stammer which showed under tension or tiredness. Equally important to his future, he gained an insight into the care of these tiny groups.

At the age of 15, sitting in his room one morning, he had a vision. Long afterwards he recalled it:

'I saw myself at a small chapel-type building, but instead of a door there was a brick wall. I found myself hammering at the brick wall with my fists, trying to get in. Suddenly the whole building collapsed inwards. The walls became individual bricks, and they rolled together into one large ball and moved away from me. I followed, to find that the bricks had been constructed into a large cathedral-type building, and I was inside shoring up the work.

'By the time I left my room, I knew that my life was not my own any longer. I had a great desire to minister to people and to build up Christ's church.'

When the new minister, the Reverend Ronald Fennell, arrived Christopher immediately asked for baptism, adding the unusual request that he be allowed to give his testimony as he came out of the water. 'I want to demonstrate that preaching is to be my life's work,' the 15-year-old lad told the bemused minister.

The baptism took place and from that moment Christopher lived, studied and worked towards his goal. Friends preaching at local churches took him with them, and he often travelled on the back of a motorcycle with Vick Collyer, a welder friend, to churches around Slough and Staines. By the age of 17 he was recognized as a local youth preacher, and it was when he was speaking in his own church on one occasion that Ruth Masters, daughter of the minister of Salem Baptist Church, Hillingdon, came to play the organ. It was the start of a friendship and an effective working partnership.

With the support of his church, Christopher applied to the South Wales Baptist College at Cardiff for ministerial training. At Cardiff he was surprised to find that he was not the only student who had been converted through the ministry of Billy Graham.

Fully one-third of the student body had been influenced, in one way or another, by the evangelist. Churches in Wales had been going through a depressing period and the number of men leaving the ministry or not finishing ministerial training was causing concern. But the college principal, Ithel Jones, was well known internationally as a dynamic preacher. Church secretaries commented on the new breed of preachers coming from 'the College'.

Christopher practised his skills round the valleys of South Wales, learning to ground eternal truths in simple, everyday terms. He was in Evan Robert's country and treading on holy ground. He devoured facts about the Welsh Revival of 1904–5 from elderly survivors—and learned how to disarm the hostility shown towards himself as a representative of the church and an Englishman.

By 22 Christopher was a fully fledged minister, having received a call to Abbey Road, Northampton. By now he had a wife to share his ministry. Ruth had been keeping step with him as she went through a university course in modern languages at Bedford College, London, and a diploma course in languages and music at Cardiff. He was, he believed, the youngest minister in the whole country, but discovered that the area superintendent was not happy with his appointment, thinking him too inexperienced. Numbers had dropped in the interregnum.

What could this young David do in the face of the Philistine forces of apathy and materialism? There was only one thing he could do. He started to preach the gospel with characteristic enthusiasm.

The large church had been built as an offshoot of College Street Baptist Church—where William Carey was baptized. Christopher took for his own Carey's answer to defeatism: 'Expect great things from God, attempt great things for God.'

He was immediately tested, though. On the first Sunday after his induction the boiler broke down, and on another Sunday water dripped through the roof on to the congregation.

Christopher took a positive line. It was his job to encourage the people to pray and look to the Lord in faith, but it was also of vital importance to encourage them to do something to take a pride in the work. And if this meant organizing jumble sales, well, so be it. He knew that it was no good praying unless you were prepared to be part of the answer.

For the first twelve months he waited with bated breath for his honeymoon period with the church to finish, but in fact he had four and a half years of glorious expansion.

One day, at a gathering of the Northamptonshire Baptist Association at College Street, the meeting was being told of the imminent and inevitable closure of a small church, Grimscote Baptist Chapel. Apparently, the people had evaporated. It was the trend, they told each other.

Christopher asked what had been done about it. It was explained that lay preachers had tried to restart the services by delivering notices around the area and preaching regularly, but the pews remained empty.

'Let us at least put God to the test on this,' he said. And he outlined a plan to draw people into the church. As the nearest minister to Grimscote, Christopher had to be the one to put the scheme into action. His church secretary Stan Harris, well aware that in a hamlet of under 100 people there was no logical reason for this chapel to exist, insisted that the rest of the church must be involved. So letters were duplicated and distributed, members of Abbey Road went on door-to-door visits, services were restarted, and slowly the local people began to come back to Grimscote Chapel—and stayed. The chapel revived. An apparently hopeless situation was retrieved, and a vision began to be fulfilled.

In 1967 Northampton ministers were discussing with a team of laymen the cost of television relays from the Billy Graham Crusade at Earls Court to the ABC Savoy Cinema, trying to answer the question: 'Would it not be better if we spent the £5,000 on our own churches?'

Christopher, who had struggled with church finance himself, had his own view on the matter. 'The cost of running this campaign will be the cost of running two of our churches,' he said. In the economics of evangelism it was worth it, he told them. And so it proved. Three hundred churches took part. The eight nights of relays drew almost 14,000 people and over 700 inquirers were counselled. Channelling these new-born Christians to local churches for nurturing gave Christopher special satisfaction.

Two years later, despite the blessing at Abbey Road, Christopher and Ruth sensed it was God's time for them to move. He asked the area superintendent to put his name on the list of men seeking new appointments. Finding the right place was not so simple.

Then the secretary of Camberley Baptist Church, Ray Bates, sent an invitation. This church was smaller in numbers than Abbey Road, but when the Sunday came for Christopher to preach there was no possible doubt.

Camberley welcomed Chris and Ruth in January 1969. The Baptist church had been founded in 1812 when artisans working on the nearby Royal Military Academy at Sandhurst, 3 miles away, took over a failed Methodist chapel. Their successors enlarged it nearly one hundred years later. Now the average morning congregation was fifty-seven.

The new minister's first test was to mastermind a facelift for the church: 'My heart groans every time I come into this place—and that's before I look at the congregation,' he joked with them. Repainting was needed and Christopher worked out that seating with chairs instead of fixed pews would increase capacity by 10%. The church agreed to the changes Christopher wanted to make, and also to the costs—£4,000, a very large sum in those days.

A colour scheme in shades of green and gold was devised. The pews were pulled out and replaced with chairs. A centre aisle was opened making life easier for brides and coffin-bearers. The wooden partition was replaced with a glass screen door. The result, seating 250 people, was a setting of peace and beauty for the drama of the gospel message, and people came in growing numbers.

New development was taking place at Frimley, a nearby area where some of the Camberley members lived. The building of the M3 in the 1960s had created virtually two separate communities. The question was, should they extend the church at Camberley to cope with increasing demands from inside and outside the church, or build another church at Frimley to accommodate the new townsfolk on land already earmarked for it?

Christopher did his homework on the problem. Either project would stretch resources. They prayed and took advice, and back came the answer—*Do both!*

One of their consultants, Brigadier General D. J. Wilson-Haffenden, said: 'Why not try God?' It became their watchword as they rented premises for a church in a school at Frimley in 1973, and took on mortgage payments for a pastor's house (paid off in six years) and for a 2,000 square-foot extension at Camberley (paid for in two-and-a-half years) all cleared by gifts and donations.

Camberley members formed the nucleus of the Frimley church. From twenty-five members it grew to seventy-five, and was given its independence of Camberley in July 1982 under the Reverend Geoff Bland. By mid-1983 over half the money has been promised for the new £100,000 church—which, on a prime site, will also be a community centre on the new estate.

When, a year after the start, the Camberley church counted up its membership they found that the gaps in the ranks had been more than filled. It seemed to be a biblical principle that applied to every phrase of the Christian life—'give and it shall be given you, pressed down and running over'.

An old church was in danger of closure. The congregation, in a village of 5,000 souls, was down to six elderly people, all aged over 80. Harry Woodason, the church secretary, contacted Christopher and asked him to take over Hartley Wintney Baptist Church near Fleet in Hampshire.

Christopher was appalled at what he saw: the dry rot was so bad that the vestry floor had fallen in, and an oak beam could be squeezed like a sponge till the water ran out. A botany lecturer at the Royal Holloway College was so excited by a rare fungus he found there that he took it back to his students!

Here was the sort of challenge Christopher loved. He supplied preachers, and some of his members transferred to Hartley Wintney. Camberley men worked on the reconstruction and when a carpenter asked the minister to conduct his marriage, Christopher said, 'Yes, if you can come and help me refloor the church at Hartley Wintney.'

October 1979 marked a new beginning when the Reverend Trefor Jones came from the South Wales Baptist College to be the minister—the first the church had had since 1943. The congregation numbered twelve at this time, including children.

By the time Trefor Jones moved in 1983 there were now thirteen adult full members of the church. There had been nine baptismal services in two years and some outstanding conversions. Meanwhile the giving has increased from £10 a week to £60. Camberley pumped £18,000 into Hartley over four years—a fact which Trefor is grateful for. He says, 'The Baptist denomination has noted this pioneering work, as evidenced by a Home Mission Fund grant.'

The Berkshire Baptist Association wanted pastoral support for a chapel at Sherfield-on-Loddon, which was barely alive with two Baptist services a month. Could Camberley help? Trefor Jones started visiting the village of 1,500 people for two and a half hours a week from 1980 onwards and this produced results. Morning services were restarted in May 1980, the women's meeting met in the chapel once more, and a link with the cubs was forged. A year later an evening service was started. Early in 1983, when Chris took an evangelistic women's meeting at the church, he found a variety of people from an unmarried mother and her child to great-grannies—and even three men! Camberley continues to back the work with funds and pastoral care until Sherfield can stand on its own feet.

In 1981 the Trustees of Cove Gospel Mission, 3 miles away, asked Camberley to purchase the former Mission which had closed. Chris Russell went to see it and he realized at once the tremendous potential.

Sitting in a sea of houses was a five-year-old building with no apparent signs of dereliction, apart from one cracked pane of glass. It was being offered for £15,000, half the price of a semi. There were 18,000 people living within a mile of the building. It was a real bargain in both material and spiritual terms.

But Camberley took a little time rising to the challenge. Some felt the price was too high; some even felt it should be free. Others felt they were doing too much already and that another church should take on the work. But in the end they voted to go ahead.

Cove Baptist Church opened in August 1982, with a nucleus from Camberley. Now the church thrives, with a regular fifty-plus at morning service and over thirty in the evening, and grants are being made available from the Home Mission Fund for a pastor.

The home base is building up yet again. From an average Sunday morning congregation of fifty-seven in one church, when Christopher began, there is now an average of 300 adults over five churches, a harvest growing where once all was waste-land.

Looking round at his spiritual acres Chris the strategist and entrepreneur computes: 'In real terms, if we were doing this today it would cost a quarter of a million pounds to purchase.' If he has a problem with this it is knowing that the church expects him to be right all the time in his judgement. But faith is important too to Chris—he doesn't claim a salary and hasn't done for seven years, preferring to look to God for his own supply, while working to provide security for others.

He measures his church, however, by what it achieves as a living fellowship: 'Every church member should have a job. Also I try to encourage people to be moulded together into a group that will want to reach out and won't become so comfortable that they would close the doors to exclude others.'

His church has a budget of £25,000 a year, and gives

away about 15% of its income. The premises are in use eighteen hours out of twenty-four most days for as well as Sunday services, counselling and weeknight activities, the extension houses a playgroup, treatment centre for the disabled, an old people's day centre serving meals, all with their spiritual emphasis. There is also an office manned by volunteer church members who help with bill-paying for the elderly, giving references for the young looking for jobs, arranging activities, giving direction to those who want to offer voluntary service.

Naturally Christopher finds that work leads to yet more work. He is on several local committees, is chairman of the Baptist Missionary Society Young People's committee, is on the BMS candidates' board and chairman of the Time For God committee—a voluntary work agency supported by young people's organizations in the Church of England, Methodist, Baptist and United Reform Churches. His wife Ruth, who looks after their three children, has a complaint: 'I'm married to superman—and I'm not superwoman.'

One of the most innovative of the Russell enterprises is the Student English Holiday Club. Students from France, Switzerland, Germany and Scandinavian countries invade Camberley every summer intent on learning English. It all began in 1970, when a need for holiday cash led Christopher and Ruth to take in two foreign students. They ended up teaching as well. Flaws in the course led them to make a bold step—to start their own language school with a Christian emphasis, using church facilities.

However, things didn't always go smoothly. Many young people wrote to say that God taught them a good deal during their stay in Camberley, but others were annoyed to find themselves in a Christian environment, and so kicked over the traces.

One particular young boy caused a great deal of trouble.

So when, the next year, Christopher saw the name of this young man he almost refused to have him.

When he arrived, though, he said he had been converted and wanted to help. He later returned as a leader.

Over the past four years the language school has had 500 students a year holidaying in the area, and has set up branches at other churches in the south.

Chris and Ruth feel the pressure of this holiday work, but look on it as spiritual investment in young lives. After one such busy summer, they were handed an essay written by a departing German student. She wrote: 'I learned here another language. Not English, but the language God speaks to me in.'

Chris Russell has fulfilled his early vision and literally built up the church in a variety of ways. He says: 'The Gospel cuts across all barriers, including that of nationality. The love of Christ makes us a new nation.' He really means it.

That vision was enlarged in 1983 when links with Southern Baptists in Maryland and Alabama resulted in a group crossing the Atlantic to Camberley Baptist Church and its allied churches. Results were thrilling—conversions of 11-year-old boys up to golden grannies.

Over at Sandhurst Christian Fellowship, 3 miles away, the Reverend John Hiron has helped Chris with the holiday language work for teenagers.

Recently the two ministers found they had a common starting-point. John's moment of enlightenment came at Harringay when he was 16. 'Within six months I knew I wanted to preach.'

Christopher certainly understands this compulsion, has a preaching team in his congregation and is training two other young men who are thinking about the ministry. He knows how God can use youthful energies.

This was forcefully brought home to him in 1978: 'There

was a ring on the doorbell and there stood a lady, who had come all the way from Australia to tell me that she found Christ through my testimony at my baptism all those years ago.'

*'We need to be the kind of church which stays present in the neediest areas and continues to believe and worship'* (David Sheppard).*

# I I

# *For God—And England*

You are batting with the England captain in a Test match at Lord's. Your eyes are on your partner as he prepares to face the ball. With masterly ease he drives the delivery through the covers for four. The scoreboard registers that England has gone ahead. You are just about to face the first ball of the next over when...you wake up. It is only a dream....

And yet, Brian Seaman woke up to find that part of his dream had come true. He was indeed batting with former England Test captain David Sheppard, and savouring the thrill of every ball. The occasion was not a Test match, though, and the ground wasn't Lord's: it was a village green in Sussex and a game between the village team and a team from the Mayflower Family Centre in East London, where the England cricketer was Warden.

To Brian, a social science student observing the workings of the Mayflower Centre, that game, in the late 1950s, was a revelation of reality beyond the sociologist's

---

*\* Bias to the Poor*, Hodder & Stoughton 1983.

power to explain, and a pointer to his own future in an inner-city ministry.

Brian would not have been there to record the scene at all, had he not, on a wet night in May 1955, taken a ride on a coach to Wembley to hear Billy Graham.

Ordinary Seaman Seaman, home on leave, was invited, with his girlfriend, to join the party going from St Mary's Church, Bexley in Kent. He wasn't interested in religion—he paid a visit to Sunday school in childhood, developed measles afterwards and quarantined himself out of the church's reach from that time onwards. The vicar, Mr Hooper, whom he scarcely knew, had once challenged him, audaciously, about playing cricket on Sunday. He took no notice, yet the incident stuck. So what was he doing here, with a coachload of St Mary's members, going to listen to some American preacher? Well, at least it was a cheap outing.

Up to that moment Brian's experience had been that life was a necessary compromise between what one wanted and what one could have. He had failed to get a scholarship—but had passed an entrance exam. He played for the Association of Kent Cricket Clubs—but had failed the Kent County Trials. He was no academic high-flier—but he'd ended up captain of the school. His hard-working and success-oriented parents wanted him to go to university, but he failed to get there. However, he had a place waiting at Loughborough College to train as a physical education teacher, after National Service. To one who was never happier than with a bat in his hand that was a cause for rejoicing rather than dismay.

Yet there was a sense of incompleteness about his life. A rather introverted lad, an only child, he wanted to be a success—even win some of the glittering prizes, but there was still a lack to which he had never given a name.

As he listened to the American preacher Billy Graham, the name came: Jesus. Jesus, that undefined childhood name and figure, suddenly became real. And called him to come.

It was as if he was hearing about him for the first time (though this was not actually the case) and somehow knew it was all true. He went forward at the end knowing clearly the right thing to do, even though he didn't have a very full grasp of the gospel itself. Brian doesn't recall having a sense of guilt at the time, but he was convinced about Jesus and that he needed him.

He didn't feel anything very deeply afterwards, nothing to indicate a change. And he wasn't followed up before he rejoined the Mediterranean fleet in Malta, where he finished his National Service in HMS *Forth*, a submarine depot ship, and rose to the rank of Leading Seaman Seaman, which wasn't funny on the lips of a Chief Petty Officer out for blood.

But there had been a change, a quiet takeover by an indwelling presence. The chief outward sign was that he began to meet regularly with two other Christians to say compline in the ship's chapel before bed, to the music of the sea. After a while he linked up with the Connaught, a Methodist group in Valletta, Malta, and then with a fellowship group and Sunday worship at the Anglican Cathedral of St Paul's, where he was confirmed.

There was good news from home too. His mother who, in Sunday school days had been given half a crown for 'giving her heart to Jesus', woke up from her long sleep and started to practise her faith.

One important consequence of this was that she started to attend lunchtime services at St Mary-le-Bow, Cheapside, London (the 'Bow Bells' church), near her work. Brian later met the vicar, Hugh Evan-Hopkins, who planted the idea of ordination after the navy.

That would mean going to university. Impossible, he thought in view of his early failure. But he was amazed at how easily it all happened.

A three-year course at St John's College, Durham, was followed by two years studying for a Diploma in Theology at Cranmer Hall.

Within a month of being demobbed Brian found himself among a crowd of men once more, many of whom were training for the ordained ministry. He attended a selection conference in his second year—and the green light came. In the space of two or three years a dramatic change had taken place and his life was under new management.

The Christian Union at Durham had the right compost. Its members were Bible-loving, lively people. Another turning point was a college mission to a parish in the south-east, where he discovered for the first time the joy of leading others to faith in Christ.

Serving on the Christian Union executive committee as prayer secretary brought him in contact during his last year with its vice-president, Marion. At first they were friends, then, towards the end of his diploma course, with academic work virtually finished, they fell in love. That posed a problem for Brian, since he was about to leave, whereas she had another year to go in reading botany.

Was she the Lord's choice as a life partner? Should he continue to see her when he left Durham?

Brian and Marion usually met at the evening service at St Nicholas. So he prayed that if she were the Lord's choice then they would meet on the following Sunday evening, which was to be his last. However, Marion wasn't in church and Brian was somewhat crestfallen. But the evening wasn't yet over. He went back to his room in college and waited to see the Lord's will.

Then the clock of Durham Cathedral began to chime the strokes of nine o'clock. Women were not allowed into the college after nine on weekends, so he knew she wouldn't come now. But suddenly there were footsteps, and as the clock struck there was a knock at the door. There stood Marion!

It was soon clear to both of them as they walked and talked in the Cathedral Close that the Lord had brought them together. Later that summer Brian proposed and they were engaged the following Christmas.

He says today, 'As with getting to university, so it was with finding a wife. My own efforts were abortive, but when I submitted my life and future to the Lord his purposes unfolded surely and smoothly.'

The seeds of a call to take the gospel to the disadvantaged inner urban areas rather than to the comfortable suburbs were sown at Durham, in his second year, when the social studies department arranged his summer practical work at the Mayflower Family Centre, Canning Town. They could hardly have chosen a better place for Brian—both a new Christian and a keen cricketer. The Mayflower had been running then less than a year and David Sheppard, one day to be Bishop of Liverpool, was the warden.

Youth work grew quickest to start with at the Mayflower, as in most churches. The older teenagers had a cricket team and Brian, inevitably found himself in it. They would go off, typical East End kids, with David Sheppard and Brian, down into some picturesque middle-class Sussex village, where they would play other teams of fairly well-to-do people. Brian usually found himself batting at the other end to David. It was a great help to his own play and a general thrill all round.

Most of the Mayflower team consisted of lads from the youth club, complete with boots and jeans, but David Sheppard—known as 'Skipper'—always turned out in his England whites and gave his best to the game.

Brian's link with the Mayflower Centre developed over the following years into a calling to join the staff. Eventually, after ordination and a first curacy spent in the inner suburbs of Manchester, at St Margaret's Church, Burnage, he became Chaplain at the Mayflower, moving in with Marion and their daughter to a terraced house in Canning Town.

It took some adjusting to the personal implications of this new life. Although Brian's parents came from a solid working-class background, by the time he was born they had climbed the social scale and now saw themselves as middle class. So he had a fair amount of adjusting to do when he and Marion went to the Mayflower. It was a real culture shock. Marion's parents became anxious when the young couple announced they were going to Canning Town, but Marion never fought it for one moment, always accepting that her husband's call to urban parishes included her and the children.

Ten years at the Mayflower marked Brian and Marion for life, in a job calling for intuitive, sensitive leadership in pastoral matters while working with a team of outstanding Christians.

It was there that they learnt that some of their middle-class interpretations of the Gospel were not appropriate. George Burton, youth leader at the Mayflower when they arrived, was a great influence on Brian's life at this time, because he was so unorthodox. He would take out his little car and they would drive around the local streets, stopping if they saw a group of people or an individual he was after. Then he would say, 'Let's pray'—and he would, right there in the car, on the street. (That was the first time Brian saw prayer as something that could happen anywhere and not just as a set-piece activity.) George would then launch off after this person or people, and would immediately start talking about Jesus in an open and bold way, in a manner quite unfamiliar to Brian. It challenged him to speak about Jesus openly, and he learned a great deal from George, both on prayer and Christian witness.

There was a large staff at the Mayflower—eleven of them including wives—and they spent quite a bit of time together. One of the key facts of their lives was the closeness. There were weekly staff meetings, then every so often they would spend a full day out together to hammer out the important issues. Crises happened all the time. Brian spent a lot of his day visiting, making contacts with local homes, sometimes taking home meetings.

They started home groups and 'searching groups' because they felt that evangelism really worked better in homes. There was full-scale youth work humming along, particularly in the late afternoon and early evenings, and there was also a nursery school.

Their next move, in January 1975, was back into parish life in one of Newcastle's inner-city areas, Elswick, where working-class people with Geordie accents had problems similar to those in Canning Town, and put the same cultural distance between themselves and 'the church'—except for occasional rites of passage, such as weddings, baptisms and funerals. The challenge was to put into practice lessons learned at the Mayflower, but without that supportive community around them. For the most part Brian and Marion found themselves facing an uphill missionary task, presenting Jesus to people who tend to repel boarders, particularly if from the South.

They found that Elswick presented many problems by virtue of its situation. What was primarily a middle-class suburb of Newcastle in the thirties, suffered inevitable inner-city decay and fell to the bulldozer.

It has three council estates, some Housing Association accommodation, as well as two primary schools, several pubs and an Alcoholic Rehabilitation Unit. The absence of private housing has an effect on church life.

Services at Brian's church, St Paul's, are a mixture of formal and informal. In winter they are held in the converted church vestry, because of the costs of heating the main building, and this tends to bring people into a closer sense of fellowship. There are about forty plus communicants, with a crèche for smaller children so mothers can now come. Sometimes lay-readers preach, and there has been a real attempt to get lay-people involved in the various aspects of the church's ministry. People are not afraid of calling things out in the notices and the atmosphere is warm and friendly.

Yet despite such progress, Brian knows that there is still not one complete Elswick family in the parish where the couple are both Christians and members of St Paul's. Response is seen in the small steps that people take, rather than in the giant leap.

Brian says, 'Some have made a profession of faith but for many the step of commitment has been too big. Evangelism in the inner city is harder than in suburbia. For historical reasons the British working class doesn't respond to the gospel, by and large. The church has done a great deal of sowing and not much reaping—but we stick at it believing there will be a harvest. We have had to adapt our method a bit.'

At St Paul's they don't put their hopes so much in religious meetings—the most fruitful work has been done in homes, pubs and community groups, where they have met people on their own ground.

That kind of setting means that people can ask the questions they want to ask, and as a result some of the people on the fringes have come fully into church life. The local pub, appropriately called The Rock, is the venue for a monthly men's meeting, when a group of up to a dozen men, a minority of whom are church members, get together with Brian—and Tony Adamson, the curate—to discuss Christian topics, such as life after death or what God says about some relevant social issue, like unemployment, to get people round to thinking seriously about Jesus and the Christian faith.

Brian and Tony, both converts of one evangelist's message, 12 years apart, are as totally unlike as any vicar and curate could be, yet they complement each other in their working relationship. Tony is a Geordie, raw and unstoppable, happier with folk on the fringe than with traditional church members, preferring to take his wife and kids when he goes visiting, and ready to hump furniture when called on. Tony was converted in a television relay from Earls Court to Newcastle City Hall in 1967 at the age of 17. He has been working as a training officer for Mission England North-East 50% of his time.

St Paul's church members are involved in serving the local community in many areas of need: through the church school, a project employing a worker among the local Asian population, work with the unemployed and with local community groups. People need to be introduced to God in a way that is relevant to their overall needs in life. Marion, who works as a Home Tutor for the LEA, has seen how the prospect of almost certain unemployment shapes young people's perceptions of themselves:

'Almost no-one can get a job so they don't talk in terms of what they will do, but in terms of "something for today or tomorrow".'

The value of Brian's long-term experience of work in inner-city areas is generally recognized both within the diocese and outside it. He was made a Canon of Newcastle Cathedral in 1982; he has served on the Newcastle Diocesan Inner City Commission; and is a member of the Scargill House Council. More recently he has become chairman of the Inner City Task Group for Mission England North East, and from this vantage point can see the value of the Mission's emphasis on the building up of the local church. The courses being run are excellent training material for parish needs and his hope is that they will equip the local Christians with a rounded view of their faith and church. Prayer is at the centre of Mission England strategy, Prayer Triplet groups are in action, and daily prayer is held in the church, with up to half a dozen members attending. The church is seeing its importance, and so are Brian and Marion.

So could a harvest time really come to inner-city Elswick with all its problems? Brian gives a qualified assent:

'We realize the need for the big meetings so that people who have been to home groups have the challenge to commitment, and we are praying that there will be some reaping from all the sowing that has been done here over the years.

'God drew me to himself without much apparent pre-evangelism, and kept me without a lot of follow-up. Since God has acted so definitely in my own life—conversion, call to service, marriage—I believe he will work in and change many other unlikely lives.'

*'You can't judge an apple in June, you have to wait till September or October'* (Billy Graham).*

# 12

# Who's That Knocking on Your Door?

Susan Watson opened the door one Saturday morning to find a lady standing there. The lady smiled sweetly and said:

'Would you be interested to buy a magazine which tells you how you can live for ever?' She held out a copy of the *Watchtower*. She was a Jehovah's Witness.

Susan was busy. The baby needed feeding. The house was a wreck. Her husband would soon be home for lunch. She really had no time, yet the words from her Bible reading that morning came to her strongly: 'Hear the word at my mouth, and give them warning from me...' (Ezek 3:17, AV). She felt that she had no excuse, so she opened the door wider and asked her in.

Susan made her some tea and they sat in the front room and she talked about Jesus and the difference he made to her life when she found him one night in 1966 in Leicester when she was a tearaway teenager, with a self-destructive outlook on life.

* *Decision*, May 1981.

153

## Susan Watson's story:

My parents, Joe and Beryl Maltby, started married life in Nottingham. Dad was first a fireman and then a plastics engineer and Mum worked part time as an overlocker in a factory in order to help make ends meet.

We moved into a new council housing estate, the Clifton estate, when I was about 4. Dad, who had never had any interest in religion up to then, started to get involved with a new church on the estate, and helped with the Boys' Brigade movement, connected with the church. He used to go canoeing and orienteering with the boys. He was christened aged 30 but it took another few years and a trip to India to show him that he wasn't really a Christian.

Dad got a job in India as a plastics engineer with an Indian firm, and he took us with him (my brother Ricky was born when I was 7). However, it didn't turn out to be the job he had hoped it would be and while he was feeling very low we met some American missionaries, John and Leona Garrison.

John and Leona were 'faith' missionaries at the time, supported by a small church in Canada. It was during a time of struggle and trouble for them, when they were left without a roof over their heads, that Mum said she could see the difference between Leona and herself: Mum was complaining, while Leona was trusting God for each moment. Realizing Leona wasn't 'normal', started Mum inquiring about the things of God.

John Garrison led Dad to know the Lord Jesus as Saviour one night in their flat. He spoke to him on Joseph, and Dad repented and believed. Mum saw the difference in Dad when he came home that night.

Mum went into her room and knelt by her bed: 'Lord, whatever Joe's got, give it to me,' she prayed. And he did. She was different too.

It was all a bit surprising for me. I was 12 by this time. I had been to Sunday school for a couple of years on the Clifton Estate, but after my parents' conversion I went to a Bible class in Leona's flat and can remember learning verses of Scripture and singing songs. I was also confirmed in Bombay Cathedral. I had an awareness of God and meant everything that I promised at the time.

During that year in India I went to the Bombay Scottish Orphanage High School, where I was the only English girl in the school. I had a Hindu friend called Shoba Wadwar, who prayed to a god called Elephanta.

'Shoba, how can you pray to a statue?' I said once, with a giggle. 'It isn't alive or anything. It can't hear you.'

But Shoba got a bit annoyed and replied quite sharply: 'How can you pray to a God you can't see?' I had no answer for that.

When we came home from India I attended the secondary modern school at Enderby, Leicester. This was a time when I became very difficult and rebellious. My friends at school were the same. I smoked—and lied about it to my mother—and bleached my hair. My friends and I drove around in a mini-bus full of lads, and my parents would have been far from pleased had they known some of the things that went on.

By this time I hardly spoke to my parents, except to quarrel. They just kept believing and praying for three long years while I went through my terrible, traumatic teens.

At school I struggled academically, desperate to leave as soon as possible, and didn't in the end take any exams. But I went to catering college and gained my City and Guilds Certificate and later became a cook in an old people's home in Kirby Muxlow, and then in Leicester.

When I was 16 my parents opened our home for Christian fellowship and meetings. They got the fellowship to pray for me then, but I wouldn't go near any of them.

A year later, in 1966, Billy Graham came back to England, and I was invited by some people in the fellowship to go with them to Granby Hall in Leicester, to the television relays from the Crusade at Earls Court. I decided to go—just to see what it was all about. I listened to the preaching and for the first time it struck home to me that I was not a nice person: I was selfish, rebellious and sinful in God's sight. At the appeal I was sitting there, my heart pounding, wondering what to do, when I heard a quiet voice say in my heart 'Go forward'. I had never heard the Holy Spirit speak before. It was so quiet and tender, but I knew if I didn't obey I would lose something precious that was being offered at that moment.

I sat for a few minutes and then someone else in our group went forward so I took courage and went as well. Alone with God, I was not conscious of anyone else, and when Billy Graham prayed with everyone who came forward something happened to me that made me different in the way my parents had become different in India. Jesus came into my life, cleansed me and made me white within and I am still thrilled with the wonder of it.

In the counselling room a man gave me a couple of scriptures to learn. One was 'God so loved the world that he gave his only begotten Son, that whosoever believeth in him should not perish, but have everlasting life' (Jn 3:16, AV). Another one was 'Resist the devil, and he will flee from you' (Jas 4:7, AV). From that time everything was new to me. The grass was greener because now I knew its Maker, the birds' songs were lovelier. The Bible was now relevant to me. When I next lit a cigarette it nearly choked me. I have never wanted one since. Jesus gave me a clean mind and a clean tongue. Hallelujah. All was forgiven.

When I married my husband, Malcolm, we moved to Barwell in Leicestershire, where I worked as a canteen manageress in a shoe factory. Then we started a family;

we now have three lovely girls and all have given their lives to the Lord.

My thoughts came back to the Jehovah's Witness lady in my front room. She talked about God and Jesus as if they were separate beings. I thought of God, my Father to whom I prayed for all my needs, and who watched over all of us. I thought of Jesus, my Saviour, friend, the living presence with me day by day, and I thought of the Holy Spirit, who filled my life with the power to live the life God wants, and taught me through the Bible. I started to tell her that God was the triune God: God the Father, God the Son and God the Holy Spirit. By this time she was getting very uneasy.

'Look,' she said suddenly, 'can I come back in a week's time with my son? There are some people waiting for me on the corner of the street and I don't have time to stay right now.' I agreed, wondering what I had let myself in for.

I prayed and asked the Lord to use me to speak to her son when he came, and to Ada his mother as well.

Ada's son, John Bevins, was tall and dark and sounded as though he knew his stuff, but I said what I had to say first. He just sat there and listened to everything that I had got to tell him about Jesus being a personal Saviour and then went away. He came back a few times, and we talked some more and went through some of the things that the Jehovah's Witnesses believe. They think that Jesus Christ is just one of God's creatures, a chief angel, and that through him God created all other things. It seemed to amaze him to find that eternal life is open to everyone, and it's not just for the 144,000 alone. You can't divide up the people of God into classes: if you are saved, you are saved.

One day, eighteen months later, he came back and with a hesitant air said:

'I can hardly believe it's happened, but I know Jesus like you do now.'

After all those months of inquiring and worrying and doubting, he had crossed over into God's kingdom by faith in Jesus Christ's finished work. The teaching of Jehovah's Witnesses is so binding that it takes a lot to cut the knots. Then his Mum also became a Christian. After this, though, the trouble started for him. His wife was against his new faith—she thought it was from the devil and that I was a wicked angel. In the end they excommunicated him from the Jehovah's Witnesses. It was a hard time for him, but eventually his wife followed him as well. With God nothing is impossible.

He brought his wife June round to meet me, and I was astonished at the change. Before, she wouldn't even look at me or speak, and now it was just as if we were in the same family.

'Isn't it wonderful to know Jesus?' She was bubbling over with the joy of it. I thanked God again that I had found the time that day to be a 'Jesus Witness'.


**John Bevins's story:**

Both my mother and I were living at Barwell, 2 miles from Hinckley, Leicester, in 1971, when I met Susan. My mother called on her first, and as she was getting a bit out of her depth she asked me if I would go along to give her some moral support.

I just took it as another routine 'back call'. I made sure I had a comprehensive selection of literature in the bag, so I was prepared for anything. But when we got there and Susan asked us in, straightaway something struck me about her attitude. She was young and obviously very kind and gentle. She made us feel very welcome and showed us friendship. That doesn't often happen to

Jehovah's Witnesses. Normally people try to get rid of them as quickly as possible.

So we sat down. I had my bag of books ready, but I never took anything from it. Susan just swept all that aside. Not in any impolite way; she just wanted to tell me about her relationship with Jesus. We never got on to doctrines or interpretations, or eschatology or the sort of things I would have normally talked about. She just wanted to tell me that to have Jesus in your life was what it meant to be a Christian.

This was a new angle to me. I had never viewed Christianity in this light. To me Jesus was somebody 'up there'. He had a function in God's plan of salvation, the chief of which was that he laid down his life that people might be saved. It was legally necessary for him to do this to satisfy God's justice, but the idea of him actually coming down by his Spirit and dwelling in the hearts of believers had never occurred to me.

It was Susan's glow that was so persuasive—it spoke louder than any arguments I could bring to bear. She seemed energized with power as she spoke of the new birth:

'Don't you see, we have to be changed inwardly before we can please God,' she said. 'You know the Bible says "Therefore if any man be in Christ he is a new creature: old things are passed away; behold all things are become new."'

'But surely this is only for the small number of Christians who will be with Christ in the heavenly kingdom—not the others,' I objected, fighting to keep a grip on the interpretations I had been taught.

But Sue drove right over them: 'Are there any others?' Sue replied. 'My Bible tells me that if I don't have the Spirit of Christ I don't belong to him. The apostle Paul said "Christ is in you except ye be reprobates." Either you're saved or you're not!'

I realized then that I had not learned the whole story, as a Jehovah's Witness. The object of my religion was to be saved by obedience to Jehovah's requirements. Foremost was the witnessing work (being a Kingdom 'publisher'), followed by attendance at all meetings where possible and participation as appropriate. Conformity to biblical standards of morality was assumed and avoidance of 'worldly' practices encouraged. The aim of all these disciplines was to be counted worthy to be allowed entrance into the 'new heavens and new earth'. This was salvation by good works, but that I could know God and walk with Christ, was something I never was aware of until I met Susan.

I had been drawn into the Jehovah's Witnesses through my interest in religion. As a boy I went to an Anglican church and sang in the choir, and attended Bible class. It was, as I recall, a pretty dead church.

After doing national service in the RAF I went back to my old job as a railway booking clerk. I had a colleague who was a Jehovah's Witness and his faith came first in his life. Our friendship grew and I often visited his house. We went through the Bible from cover to cover and though I had many doubts about interpretations, so many of the passages had uncanny relevance to what I was seeing in the world around me. The Bible came out of the realm of history into the present.

I met my colleague in May and by August I was doing a regular study on the Watchtower books. It was twelve months after that that I started going around with him on his door-to-door work. Then in April 1960 I was accepted into the Kingdom Hall. I made the usual progress, becoming a Servant (Deacon) in 1967, and I married a Jehovah's Witness, the daughter of a zealous member of the sect. I was right into it. My mother was undoubtedly influenced by me when she also became a witness in 1966.

The Jehovah's Witnesses publish a little book—*The Truth That Leads to Eternal Life*. When I went to see Susan I had a copy of this in my bag, and I was all ready to get a weekly home Bible study going with her if she was willing. But this young woman floored me. The bag never opened.

I used to go back quite frequently. On Sunday mornings when we went on door-to-door work, if we had half an hour to spare before lunch, I'd go there. I'd talk about 'the last days'—the dreadful state of the world, God's coming judgement. Sue would come back with:

'Yes, but do you know Jesus?'

No, I didn't. As if trying to discover some secret formula I would ask:

'And just how do you get to know Jesus?'

'Have you tried praying to him?' She'd be smiling as she said this.

Pray to Jesus? Heresy! How could he ever find a way into my heart?

One Sunday morning Sue's mother and father were there. Her mother once said, 'You very often find that people who are very strong on doctrine are very deficient in love.' I couldn't help but think, 'How true that is. You can be so meticulous in getting the answers right, but your actual relationships with other people can be so cold.'

With Sue there was a reaching out to me, yet she wasn't doing it in an obvious manner. She was showing me spiritual truth and God was reaching me through her.

About eighteen months after I first met Susan I came to my own moment of new birth. I was in my room trying to pray, but it was as if my mind had been switched off. As I struggled for words it was as if I saw a vision of a dark creation. Then the glory of God filled it. I saw myself as utterly sinful, and without any hope. Over the next three days I thought about my problem, and the gulf that existed between me and God and whenever I did I found that Jesus was coming more and more into my thoughts. I saw that he was the answer to my problem. He had borne my sin and bridged that gulf, and all the Bible knowledge I had now made sense to me in a real and living way. That was in February 1973.

I started to go to the mid-week meetings at the evangelical church in Hinckley. I learned how false were some of the doctrines I had absorbed from the Jehovah's Witnesses, but lacked the courage to confess my faith and break away.

That summer I took the family to Ilfracombe for a holiday. It really hit June hard when on the Sunday I went to the evangelical church in the morning, and with her to the Kingdom Hall in the afternoon:

'You're a hypocrite. How can you have a foot in two camps?' she cried. She couldn't understand what had happened to me, and it upset her badly that I should be playing the traitor like this.

Eventually, I had to face the music. I knew I couldn't go on having a foot in both camps. Someone saw me coming out of the Wednesday night prayer meeting at the evangelical church, and took the news back to the Kingdom Hall. So then there was an inquisition. I couldn't deny the experience I had had.

The elders tried to argue with me but eventually they disfellowshipped me, announcing to the congregation that I was guilty of 'conduct unbecoming to a Christian'. No explanation other than that. All I had done was become a real Christian.

The Jehovah's Witnesses won't call on us now. June was speaking with our window-cleaner, who is a Jehovah's Witness, recently and told him of our former association with the Watchtower Society. She added gaily, 'I hope that doesn't mean you won't clean our windows any more!'

The next day we had a note through the door, 'Dear Madam, I won't be cleaning your windows any more. Very sorry.' They don't forget or forgive.

After my conversion I told my story in an article in the *Evangelical Times*. A Jehovah's Witness lady wrote to me because I had used the name of Jehovah at the end of it—'The blessing of Jehovah, it maketh rich; and he addeth no sorrow therewith' (Prov 10:22, ASV). I ended up having quite a correspondence with Alice Stansfield of Morecambe and finally she too became a Christian. She witnessed at her Kingdom Hall and others left the movement.

Jehovah's Witnesses spread their doctrines through literature. At the time I left the quota for 'Kingdom publishers' (i.e. ordinary members of the congregation) was to sell 12 magazines per month. A 'pioneer' who does 100 hours a month is supposed to sell 100 a month. I went on to help send out literature that has the power to persuade towards the truth, and to win hearts and minds for Jesus Christ. But it needs human beings to plant the message, and to back up the printed word by their caring, concerned lives.

**Alice Stansfield's story:**

I was a Jehovah's Witness for thirty-six years, living under the fear of Armageddon. Yet I had many questions about some of the doctrines I had been taught. I found in the Bible that Christians have a heavenly hope, not an earthly hope, as the Jehovah's Witnesses make one believe. They say that heaven is reserved for the 144,000, but I read in Revelation 7:4 (which is what they base it on) that the 144,000 are Jews. They say that God has cast off the Jews, because they have rejected Christ but I was pondering on

Romans 11, which says they will never be cast off.

So I thought, 'They're wrong on this!' I tried to go over it with the Witnesses, but they somehow managed to turn it.

One day I found a tract under my car windscreen, 'An Open Letter to Jehovah's Witnesses' which confirmed my doubts.

I went to the local Christian bookshop and found books on Christianity. Then I was handed a copy of the *Evangelical Times*' special issue about Jehovah's Witnesses who had been converted. I wrote to John Bevins because he had used the word 'Jehovah'.

John wrote me a simple, kind letter and the correspondence lasted several months. He told me how he had become a Christian. He took me as far as he could by letter, then he suggested that I contact a local minister and talk to him personally.

The minister couldn't help me but I heard about a Bible teaching convention on 'Life in the Spirit'. By the time I came home from that my chains, forged by the Watchtower movement, had fallen off and Jesus came to be the guest in our home.

About twelve months after, my husband was converted, after twenty-nine years as a Witness. My mother of 92 (a Witness for thirty-four years) also returned to the Lord. She had been converted at 18, but got married and back-slid. Twenty people who were associated with the Watchtower movement have left through my testimony. At least three families among them have become true Christians.

So much time was wasted in the Watchtower movement. Now I go door to door talking about Jesus. It is hard, but important, and I am surprised that more churches don't do it.

*'Jesus teaches the victorious assurance that God answers every true prayer'* (Billy Graham).*

# 13

# *Night of Miracles*

Verena Wood sat at the piano and willed herself to play the notes of her practice piece. Her hand was swollen and every movement to stretch the octave gave agonizing pain. Tears gathered in the 12-year-old's eyes. What was happening to her? Grade 4 (internal) was looming and those sharp-eared professors at the London College of Music would know if she missed practice. She might even lose the junior scholarship for which she had worked so hard. Verena thought of the other talented youngsters in her Saturday morning classes, all, like her, beavering away at instruments for the chance of a place on the concert platform one day, with hard work and supreme good luck. All this trouble because of a silly tumble out of bed.

Once more Verena tried—and was answered with an excruciating pain. She could not stretch her fingers at all. The swollen wrist throbbed. The distraught child snatched the music from the piano, flung it across the room and burst into tears.

*Decision*, January 1983.

165

But Verena's troubles were only beginning. A check-up with the doctor and a new set of X-rays of the wrist revealed unsuspected serious damage from that fall out of bed three months before. Mother and daughter heard, aghast, that the scaphoid bone was broken in five places—a comminuted fracture they called it—and the pieces had partly healed, but were out of alignment. It was goodbye to the piano and to her scholarship classes for some time to come, while the fractures were reset.

Goodbye for ever. In spite of the doctors' best efforts arthritis set in. It was a bitter time for her.

Verena's world was shattered, as, not being able to stretch the octave she had had to give up her music training. Her disability got worse and, by the time she was 16 she couldn't cut up her food, comb her hair or write with a pen. She left school wondering what on earth she should do with her life.

So there she was—a bright young girl on the threshold of life carrying a useless wrist in a plaster cast and a weight of questioning in her heart. What had she done wrong, she thought, that God should be punishing her like this? Why give her the gift of music, only to take it away so cruelly?

It seemed such a waste, a tragedy. Yet Verena had the courage to fight back. She found a job that would take account of her disability, as a trainee dispenser at Boots. Cortisone injections went some way to controlling pain, and helped her to use the wrist a little but made her put on weight, and her mouth felt perpetually dry. She felt fat, ugly and useless.

Verena's parents were Christians. They told her that she was a miracle baby—an answer to prayer after nine childless years. She had felt cared for and precious, knowing how much they loved her. Now came sliding in the serpent thought that all this love had not been enough to protect her against disaster. The miracle had turned sour and her mother's God did not really care—or else did not really have any power to help.

In a mood of cynicism and bitterness Verena locked away the glorious company of Bach and Beethoven, excused herself from family prayers when she could, and covered her walls with Beatles posters. The house rocked with pop music—*and* with Verena's temper when asked to turn it down.

Wild horses would not have dragged Verena to hear Billy Graham at Earls Court on June 28th 1967 but for a particularly bad bout of pain that kept her home from work. The stubborn pain would not let go. Verena was bored stiff with it and with herself. Also, frankly, she was a little bit curious about this Billy Graham. She had been reading *Decision* magazine.

People around her at Earls Court seemed so happy that her misery locked her in. She was only half listening to the preacher—a trick learned at meaningless church services.

But Billy Graham's words cut into her thoughts with startling force:

'You may have come from a Christian home. You may have read the Bible every day and prayed, but it doesn't make you a Christian. You have to make your own decision for yourself.'

Verena sat up. She had arrived feeling 'all right' because of her Christian home, now the words from the preacher threw her into confusion.

It was like a window opening on a new landscape, filled with light and love. It was for her—if she would take the step of faith. She knew she could not hide from God behind her parents' beliefs any longer.

At the appeal she got out of her seat and joined the crowds flocking to the counselling room and made her decision to follow Christ and to trust him with her whole life, even in the face of this ever-present pain. The wonder of the moment never left her:

'I can remember feeling very, very unworthy of the Lord's love, and in tears I truly did repent of "the years that the locusts had eaten", not only in a spiritual sense but in a physical sense as well. As I went home I had a great feeling of having every burden lifted off me. The joy was incredible.'

She was lifted by the joy of the crowds singing on the tube trains on their way home from Earls Court. She sang with them.

Her parents noticed the difference immediately—it was as if a light had been switched on in their daughter's life. Her temper vanished and Bach and Beethoven replaced the Beatles on the record player.

St Mildred's Church, Lee, South London, had been a quiet, somewhat ordinary place until the vicar, Reg Sanger, a sound evangelical, turned charismatic six years after his arrival through the influence of the renewal movement. In 1968 he started to preach in a totally different way, and the young people were the first to respond. Eventually, in about 1977, he did away with the choir stalls, installed a baptistry and started baptizing by immersion.

Before conversion Verena had been an intermittent and bored churchgoer, but with new life she was drawn to attend more regularly. Her aunt, knowing her love of music, told the vicar and the next week the vicar tackled her about joining the choir. So Verena came fully into the life of the church, in a most enjoyable way, through music.

There one morning, after her first communion, Verena spoke in tongues. It was a natural response to the joy that flooded her on the night of her conversion, and which was still there, bubbling away inside.

In April of that year she went for one of her periodic check-ups and got some shattering news: 'We could operate, but it will only postpone the day when your hand will be completely useless. Just start training yourself to do everything with your left hand.'

It was a terrible bombshell. 'Where are you, Father?' she asked. 'I'm only in my teens and my life is finished.'

Verena went to church that Sunday, April 28th, and shared it with the vicar.

He said, 'You know the Lord can do something for you, don't you?'

Verena shuffled. 'I believe he can heal other people, but I can't somehow believe he'll do it for me.'

'Go home and seek the Lord for the rest of the day and come back after evening service and tell me what he has said to you,' said the vicar.

Verena did just that, and had the words of Jeremiah 32:27 (AV) imprinted on her mind: 'I am the Lord, the God of all flesh: is there any thing too hard for me?' So after the evening service she went to the vicar and told him: 'God can heal me.'

When the time came Verena stuck out her withered hand, with its swollen knuckles, and its half a plaster cast. Reg laid hands on her and prayed, in the authority of the risen Lord. She started to thank the Lord for healing her. Her faith rose. She believed he had healed her.

Afterwards she described the moment: 'There was a lovely sensation of warmth from Reg's hands, but more so was the healing balm of peace which really seemed to pervade my whole being.'

The answer was quite dramatic. As soon as they had said their 'amens', Verena's pain disappeared. She looked at her hand. It didn't look very different, but it felt wonderful—soothed, warm. A hand again, not a lump of clay.

'It feels better,' she said, and tucked away the sling she had been wearing as a small act of faith. What happened next is something she will never forget.

As she walked along the South Circular Road with Susan and a few other friends she felt a constriction. The girls stopped under a street lamp and wrenched off the plaster. What they saw left them gazing in amazement—they saw the hand changing back to normal. The muscles were filling out. The swelling went from the knuckles. The bony look disappeared. Carefully, Verena stretched out her fingers and gently bent her wrist. Everything moved a little stiffly at first, but there was not a trace of pain. For the first time in four years it felt completely normal. The girls jumped for joy.

It was about 10.30 p.m. by then so she didn't phone Reg, her vicar, but went to see him after work the next day. She walked down the road, swinging the arm, and waved it at him as he looked at her through his window. Reg beamed with pleasure.

It was the opening of the floodgates for the adult congregation of St Mildred's, who had watched the renewal work among their young people with interest but scepticism.

By this time Verena was working at Lloyds of London—the dispensing had become impossible as her wrist worsened. Her colleagues that Monday morning were spellbound by the healing. They listened to her story without doubt or questioning.

A few weeks later Verena went for her usual check-up. The consultant was completely foxed; he took extra tests, all sorts of X-rays. By then it wasn't the house surgeon who was examining her, but the senior consultant himself.

He scrutinized all the X-rays before finally saying: 'It *is* a miracle! I can only say your God has done for you what we couldn't.'

A year later came a severe test. The church was short of an organist, and Verena was approached to help on a rota with three others.

She had never had any organ lessons, but she would try. 'For You, Father,' she whispered.

She was allowed one service a month, in the morning, when there were no psalms or canticles—just four hymns. Bit by bit the others fell by the wayside, and she was left carrying the whole lot and the choir as well.

The overcoming of the technical problems involved in playing the huge Father Willis three-manual organ, with all those stops and full bass pedal board and old wooden tracker action was, for Verena, a statement about the completeness of her healing. It was heavy work to play and had, in fact, beaten many men, but the Lord gave the strength.

As she looks back, she says of the painful turn in her life:

'If I had been allowed to continue with my scholarship music would have come first in my life. Now Jesus comes first, and I can give him back the gift of music he has given to me.'

For a special musical celebration, that first Christmas after she took over the organ and choir, Verena adapted the whole of a glorious modern cantata, 'Night of Miracles'. And as she played her way through the triumphant evening, with the choir in top voice, it was her witness to everyone that she believed in a God of miracles, and had proved his power.

*'The only true joy is living in the centre of God's will'*
(Billy Graham).*

# 14

## *The Running Man*

When Eric Delve thinks about the first twenty-nine years
of his life he remembers the running he did. Most of the
time, from about the age of 12, he was running from a
presence that was identified with a back-street Brethren
Assembly and a dour, stoic tradition of Christianity. But
the faster he ran, the shorter the rope that drew him in.

Hearing Billy Graham preach at Harringay was for Eric
the moment of realization that God and Christianity were
bigger than 'the meeting' at the hall.

He didn't know that there were that many Christians in
the entire world. The sheer shock of seeing 11,000 people
in one place and hearing them sing, was an earthquake to
him, spiritually and emotionally.

He sat there looking at Billy waving his arms about—in
those days they called him 'the human windmill'—and he
knew that an evangelist was what God wanted him to be.
But he was also conscious, as he looked at Billy, that he
could never be as good as that.

*From John Pollock, *Crusades: Twenty Years with Billy Graham*,
copyright © Billy Graham Evangelistic Association.

Most evangelists he knew were boring men with a tired message—he didn't want to be like them. He wanted to be like this vibrant man on the platform, with his power in getting a response.

Very proud and insecure, Eric decided that if he couldn't be the best, then he didn't want to know. So he went out and forgot the whole thing, and got on with growing up, which in his case meant letting the biological drive take over as he chased the girls. He was a good-looking lad—and achieved this aim with quite a degree of success.

Blundering along, with no sense of direction, he left school after O-levels and then was in and out of fourteen jobs in the next few years. Some lasted as much as six months, one lasted for two months. Shop assistant, sales clerk, fireman, advertising salesman—the list went on and on. He would get bored with a job—or his employer would tire of him.

He had, of course, a way of rationalizing his stop-go career and of silencing that small voice that tried to point him in another direction.

His justification was that he wanted to be a salesman, and that the best way to be one was to meet lots of people, and that changing his job frequently was good training for being a salesman, and so on.

In fact, although he wouldn't face up to himself, he was on the run from God. There was no rest for him.

Marriage to 17-year-old Pat from Morden when he was 21 offered a new beginning. They met through church, which Eric still attended, maintaining the belief that he had booked his seat and was 'all right'.

He says today, 'I really thought everything would be fine... heaven on earth. I was the romantic type. As soon as the marriage developed problems, I wrote it all off, in my immaturity, and reverted to my former lifestyle—chasing women. By the time I was 26 we had four children and my wife and I really hated each other.'

Pat was in a severe state of depression—partly because of the marriage but partly because of her own background. She had spent her adolescence fighting her parents and still had problems bottled up inside her. Marriage had made them worse.

About this time somebody gave Eric the name of Roger Forster, an evangelist, who was running an open home in Erith for people with similar problems. Eric contacted him, and Roger visited them.

One day he was speaking with Pat and she said, 'Oh I want to die, I want to kill myself.'

'Oh forget it. Let her kill herself and then she'll be happy and I'll be happy,' Eric retorted, raw from the chafing of the marriage bond.

The anger that met him as Roger whirled, white as a sheet, was God's anger:

'Eric Delve, that does it. I've had enough of you. I'm going, and don't call me again. I don't want to know. But before I go let me tell you this... you're going to hell.'

'I can't go to hell. I'm a Christian.' Weak, and he knew it. Back came the truth that hit the nerve:

'"Christians" who live like you do go to hell double-quick. God's got no room in heaven for hypocrites... read your Bible and start living the life.'

Roger paused at the door. 'I'll tell you something else. Not only if you died tonight would you go to hell. You'll be in hell before you die, if you go on living the way you are.' And with that he went.

The problem, as Eric sees it today, was this: 'I believed everything, and I could even quote you chapter and verse for most of it—I just wasn't prepared to live by it, to trust that God actually knew what was best for me, and let him take control.'

But Roger's denunciation pulled him up short, and he

went searching for the narrow way once more.

'Lord, I'm going to serve you...,' he promised. And he did. He and Pat started running a coffee bar for Wimbledon kids at the local church, and he got back on friendly terms with Roger Forster. But his problem was Eric Delve...there was no cure for it.

During the visit of Arthur Blessit to All Souls, Langham Place, in 1971 Eric went forward publicly.

Pat and he had gone there with the children from the coffee bar they were running at church. In the appeal Arthur seemed to be describing Eric's position. He went forward and found Pat was there beside him. He says today: 'In spite of a previous experience in 1961, it was now that she really became a Christian and began to face up to all her problems—which were massive—for which she had been taking increasing quantities of illicit drugs, just to cover up. From this time on she committed herself to stop taking drugs and she went into a Christian rehabilitation centre. As soon as they weaned her off drugs, all the problems that had been covered up so long just came bursting out.'

During the next five years Pat was in and out of hospital. Eric managed to keep the children with him, helped by a series of babysitters from the Christian Union at Froebel Institute, and a wonderful church worker called Mary, from Kensington Temple.

But Eric's own battle with God wasn't quite over. He took a job running a sales office in the West End, and it led to trouble.

He actually had an affair with a female member of staff. It was a very brief relationship, and when it was over he once again felt remorse.

He says: 'I went up on Epsom Downs, and I felt so dirty that I knelt down in the horse dung, and started to go into the routine. "I'm sorry, Lord, I won't do it again."'

But this time God spoke very, very clearly to him: 'Eric, that was your last chance. If you want Esau's choice you can have it.'

Like a piercing sword it cut through him: Esau sold his birthright for a single meal—and he found no chance to repent, though he sought it with tears. Eric knew that God was saying: 'This is it. You go on like this and you have lost your birthright.'

As he looked back he could see that his life had been a series of disasters, complete chaos, because he had refused to do the will of God. God demands a real turning from sin and a commitment to his standards.

Finally, Eric said, 'Lord, I'm going to obey you. I'll go your way.'

He was 29 and it had taken seventeen years to run full circle.

About six months after Arthur Blessit's visit, Eric was talking with Roger about a man who had been an evangelist but had given up. Eric said something flippant like, 'Jolly good job he gave up. He can go and do something useful now.' Needless to say, Roger turned round and said, 'If that man was meant to be an evangelist, then to give up is the greatest tragedy that could happen. As far as I am concerned the word "evangel" is the most beautiful word in any language, and to be an evangelist is the greatest privilege any man could ever have.'

As he was speaking, Eric felt drawn back to a night in Harringay. He saw himself watching Billy Graham, hearing his voice, looking at all the people, and knowing what God was calling him to do. He had totally forgotten it, but God carried him back there in that vision. God seemed to be saying 'I still want you to be an evangelist—I am still calling you.'

Eric cried all the way home in the car. He cried for sheer amazement and gratitude at the grace of God, that he loved him so much that he was prepared to forgive and forget all the things he had done and use him in his service.

Yet Eric had four children to support. He wrestled with this call of God. Every month it got more painful, thinking 'I'd better resign now', and yet being afraid. Eventually the boss sent for him and asked him what was the matter.

'Well, to be honest with you, I want to go and preach the gospel and I am trying to work up the courage to come and resign,' said Eric.

'I think you've just done it,' said the boss. 'Frankly, I don't want anybody here whose heart isn't in it.'

When Pat saw him walking down the road she knew. 'You've resigned!' she said as he came in.

Eric's big breakthrough as an evangelist came at the London Festival for Jesus in 1972, when he made his mark at a massive Hyde Park rally. He then became a freelance evangelist, and in 1976 joined British Youth for Christ, as its national evangelist. It was the base he needed, and his explosive talents, combined with those of Clive Calver, as national director, and Graham Kendrick, an outstanding musician, helped to move BYFC into the big league. Seven years later he could feel the push from the younger men, and he knew that he and they needed room to grow. It was launch-out time for him.

Through the years Eric has had to face the pressures and temptations that come the way of any evangelist. He can say, with humility: 'Every year some fall by the way-side, defeated by pride, sex or money. Looking back I have been amazed by the grace of God to me.'

Eric has found himself, and all the experiences gained along the way now pour out of him in vibrant illustration of the power of Christ in a human life. Recognition of his gifts is growing in Britain.

He is now a part-time tutor in evangelism at Trinity

College, Bristol and spends the rest of the time in evangelism. During Mission to London he was the principal British evangelist associated with Luis Palau. He works under a Trust and uses the title *Down to Earth* for most of his city-wide campaigns.

So what does Eric think now of the man who has served as his model all these years?

'Billy Graham has risen from being an evangelist to becoming a significant world figure. You can't do a survey of world Christianity without including Billy Graham, yet he remains one of the humblest people I have ever met. He has retained his spirituality, retained his dynamic, his singleness of purpose. He has not been side-stepped, nor let himself be bribed by better offers, he has maintained his integrity. Billy stands as an example of a man who will be obedient at all costs.

'Billy stands as a model for all men who are engaged in evangelism.'

# ·15

# *What Is This Good News?*

by

Eric Delve

**The work of an evangelist**

I have been asked more than once how one accounts for the terrific response when Billy Graham preaches—those hundreds and thousands coming out in answer to the appeal.

Billy always says this about himself, 'God has anointed me specifically for one job and that is for the appeal... to publicly call people to repentance in Christ'. The thing that marks out the evangelist who is called to that kind of ministry is this authority, which is there by the anointing of God, to call people publicly to repentance. By no means all evangelists can do it and certainly not all preachers. People respond to the invitation of a man called to call.

One of the reasons why an appeal is important is that we are social beings. 'There is no such thing as a private Christian,' said John Wesley. We all of us have to find some way of making a public stand for Christ.

In the early days of the New Testament it was impossible

for a stand for Christ to be anything other than a radical step, because you were actually pinning your faith on something that was considered heresy. To say that the emperor was not God and Jesus Christ was king—king of a hidden kingdom—made you eligible for the death penalty. You didn't commit yourself unless you meant it.

Our problem is that even in the evangelical wing of the church we have so processed the whole business of becoming a Christian that you can meet people who are solid, believing, evangelical Christians yet who still do not have any personal relationship with Christ. They gave their assent to the process without giving themselves to Jesus.

*Why is going to the front important?*
Going to the front nails to the cross the respectability of your own public persona as a rational being. It looks such a foolish act. The reason so many come to Christ in these crusades is that they are given an opportunity to make what so many of them desperately need and that is a public commitment.

The New Testament writers never intended that we should think that faith was some kind of intellectual assent. Faith was acting. Faith was obedience. 'They were unable to enter because of unbelief' (Heb 3:19, RSV). If you don't obey you have no faith. The vital thing about walking to the front is that it gives you an opportunity to actually obey God in something…to dramatize, put into action what you have already said in your head.

*What actually happens when people go to the counselling room?*
We help them to commit their lives to Christ. We tell them that it is like marriage. People can live together for years but unless they commit themselves publicly to each

other with words we don't recognize them as being married. Marriage is costly. When we get married we say: 'I promise to love you, cherish you, look after you, stick with you, even if you are poor, or sick, as long as we both shall live.' We clothe our commitment to each other with words.

In the counselling room we attempt to put clothing on the commitment people have made to Christ.

People mean different things when they come to the front at an evangelistic meeting. They may have come in a gesture of repentance, turning their backs on the old life; they may be totally ignorant of Christian doctrines, yet they may be genuinely converted at that time. We say, 'You have committed yourself to God, to Christ. This is what all that means.'

For others coming forward is a cry for help, so we tell them: 'We want you to understand that when you compare yourself to Jesus Christ you will see clearly what the Bible says about you. That you are a failure, incomplete, substandard. God means you to be like Christ. The Bible says, we are "predestined to be conformed to the image of his Son" (Rom 8:29, RSV). But the guilt of our failure comes between us and God. Jesus Christ demonstrated what we are meant to be and then died the death that was a substitution for us.

'What that death means is that God filled Jesus up with the agony of everybody who has ever suffered in this world. Filled him up with the guilt and misery, torment, the crime, greed and lust of a world gone mad. When he died the blood spilt was the sign of death. He paid the ultimate price. He died for you.

'In coming forward what you are saying is "I am willing for that sacrifice to be for me personally. I accept Jesus Christ as the one who died for me. Here and now because he died for me I receive him as my king for ever. From this

moment on I am no longer going to live for myself I am
going to live for him. He is going to take charge."'

## The purpose

We want them to recognize their failure, that Christ has
died for them, that there is only one way to live and that is
not by their own power but by his power. He must come
and live in them. The Christian life is Jesus Christ risen
from the dead, and living inside ordinary human beings,
like you and me.

## What does God do?

He penetrates to the very core of human beings. The
moment he sees the slightest trace of any part of any
human being turning towards him he rushes in with all the
love in his heart to give power to that little tiny part that
wants to repent until that becomes the principal desire of
that person. I always get people to say this prayer—'I
open myself to you'—for that is all we can do, as failures,
sinful and defiled. He comes in with the sign of the death
of Jesus, the blood, to cleanse us; he comes in to mark us
and seal us for ever with the Holy Spirit. He comes in as
Father to make us his children, to touch our dead natures
with his love. There's that marvellous phrase in 2 Corin-
thians 5:17—'If any one is in Christ, he is a new creation'
(RSV). As the Spirit of God joins with the spirit of man
there comes into being a new creature. There is a fusing—
something that has never been before. That is the New
Birth.

## Can you mistake it for anything else, and doubt it?

The experience of God coming in is so fresh, that you
can't doubt it. I always say to people, 'I don't have to
believe I'm married. I am married.' So I don't have to sit
around wondering if God exists. I know he does.

## Three steps to salvation

1. *Recognize that you are a sinner* and that there is nothing that you can do about it. 'All have sinned and fall short of the glory of God' (Rom 3:23, RSV). Jesus Christ is the standard that God has set for each one of us to attain. The Bible says we have all come short of that standard. Turning over a new leaf will not work.

2. *Turn from your sin* and turn to Jesus Christ. 'He himself bore our sins in his body on the tree, that we might die to sin and live to righteousness. By his wounds you have been healed' (1 Pet 2:24, RSV). God only requires from you the honesty to admit that you are morally and spiritually a failure. You can come to Christ just as you are.

3. *Commit yourself.* 'Jesus Christ, I believe and trust you. I believe you died for me. I give you all my sin and guilt. Thank you for forgiving me. I open myself to you. Come in now as my King and Saviour, and take charge of my life. Thank you. Amen.'

And finally, if you have found Christ don't keep it a secret. Go and tell somebody.

*Also in paperback from Kingsway . . .*

# Time to Share

## by Jim Smith

Christians have a lot to share. But even the most well-meaning find it hard at times to witness to their faith lovingly and effectively.

Jim Smith has written for those who believe in 'doing evangelism' rather than just talking about it. With his feet on the ground and his sights set on the coming kingdom, he takes us through the steps of telling others the good news of Jesus Christ.

Here we see how to

- build friendships
- share the facts
- lead someone to the Lord
- support a new believer
- learn from mistakes
- silence the Enemy.

Through it all Jim encourages us with humour, realism and the thrill of being involved in the sovereign work of God.

**A Falcon Book**
*Kingsway Publications*

# Friendship Evangelism

## by Arthur McPhee

'The best evangelism takes place in a context of mutual trust and respect. It takes place between friends.'

This book sets out to show that your greatest witness is your deepest relationship. Too often evangelism is seen as a mechanical function rather than a personal friendship. In fact our faith is something we have to **share**. If we really care about others, we must be prepared to commit ourselves to them. Good news to members of today's broken society is a loving fellowship where they will find acceptance.

Arthur McPhee's practical advice makes this a handbook on friendship evangelism for every member of the church.

*Kingsway Publications*

*Also in paperback from Kingsway ...*

# 'Lord, let me give you a million dollars'

**by Duane Logsdon** *with Dan Wooding*

**'Lord, if you really want me to give up my church pastorate and go full time into business, please let me, in return, give you back a million dollars.'**

Duane had always been able to earn a living. But when he and his wife became Christians, a Bible college training launched him into a breadline ministry of pastoring new churches. As his family grew and his income withered, Duane and his wife teetered on the brink of nervous exhaustion and marital collapse.

A hard decision confronted them. Was the pastorate the only form of 'God's work'; or was there an alternative that would not threaten their precious family life?

Then Duane met Luis Palau, and the Lord opened up a new and unexpected avenue of service that would be a blessing to thousands all over the world.

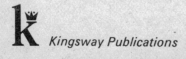

*Kingsway Publications*

# The Cross Behind Bars

*The true story of Noel Proctor—
Prison Chaplain*

## by Jenny Cooke

As a boy, Noel Proctor thought that God didn't live
outside the Sunday School classroom. Until something
happened that was to turn his life upside down and
launch him into a totally unexpected career: chaplain to
one of Her Majesty's prisons.

Noel soon discovered that he couldn't convert the
hardened inmates of Britain's prisons singlehanded.
God had to do a deeper work in his life before revival
could come to the nation's 'forgotten people'.

This is the warm and intimate account of how one man
learned to live in the power and will of God, and how his
wife found the courage to fight 'terminal' cancer. Above
all it shows how God's power can be released when his
people put him first in their lives.

**Noel Proctor** *held chaplaincies
at Wandsworth, Eastchurch and
Dartmoor Prisons before becoming
Senior Chaplain at Strangeways
in Manchester.*

**Jenny Cooke** *is an adult education
tutor who teaches creative writing.
She is married with three children.*

*Kingsway Publications*